S0-AOV-774

Overcoming the Magnetism of Street Life

Overcoming the Magnetism of Street Life

Crime-Engaged Youth and the Programs that Transform Them

Trevor B. Milton

LEXINGTON BOOKS
Lanham • Boulder • New York • Toronto • Plymouth, UK

Published by Lexington Books
A wholly owned subsidiary of The Rowman & Littlefield Publishing Group, Inc.
4501 Forbes Boulevard, Suite 200, Lanham, Maryland 20706
http://www.lexingtonbooks.com

Estover Road, Plymouth PL6 7PY, United Kingdom

British Library Cataloguing in Publication Information Available

Library of Congress Cataloging-in-Publication Data
Overcoming the magnetism of street life : crime-engaged youth and the programs that transform them / Trevor Milton.
p. cm.
Includes index.
ISBN 978-0-7391-5083-2 (cloth : alk. paper)
1. Community-based corrections—New York (State) 2. Juvenile delinquents—New York (State) 3. Juvenile corrections—New York (State) 4. Juvenile justice, Administration of—New York (State) I. Title.
HV9279.M55 2011
364.3609747—dc23 2011028184

™ The paper used in this publication meets the minimum requirements of American National Standard for Information Sciences—Permanence of Paper for Printed Library Materials, ANSI/NISO Z39.48-1992.

Printed in the United States of America

Contents

Figures and Tables

Prologue: Volatile Teens and the Social Survival Kit

This book explores the allurement of crime to a segment of today's youth. Teens throughout the United States—and in New York City in particular—are looking to a criminal lifestyle as a sustainable option when social conditions fail to produce others. On its own, adolescence is a rocky road filled with fresh impulses, poor impulse control, insatiable new indulgences, and obscene mistakes. Add twenty-first century American cultural pressure—to have the most expensive brand name clothes; or to have the latest 4G smart phone; or have the most popular club music on your playlist; or to have a checklist of sexual conquests under your belt—and this makes the life of a teenager that much more volatile.

We've all been there, every adult reading this book. From a teen's perspective, adults seem to have it all figured out. They know how to take care of themselves while simultaneously having fun. They get to drive, drink, smoke, have sex, stay out late, have their own private space—and no one is in their ear telling them how to do it. We all felt *ready* to engage in these activities well before we could legally do so. Unfortunately, exploration of adult identity requires taking risks, often times against the wishes of our caretakers. *How* we do this varies from teenager to teenager.

Adolescent deviant behavior is an inevitable part of growing up, juvenile crime a conceivable option, depending on one's circumstances. Sometimes the combination of poor impulse control and increasing social pressure leads to lawbreaking behavior. This book delves deep into the lives of several New York City teenagers who have had contact with its criminal justice system. They initially made poor choices, choices that most community members would see as intolerable, and therefore punishable. But their choices were conditioned by their environments: pressured by poverty, antagonistic "friends," overpowering enemies, overly authoritative school structures, and yes, those twenty-first century American cultural values. This is a story of crime-engaged teens from the roughest parts of New York.

Adolescents raised in impoverished conditions eventually face an arduous crossroad. These are the snap decisions that will affect their rest of their adult lives. On one path, they can travel the uphill trek through hard work, dysfunctional schooling, daily police scrutiny, lost social rewards, and generally low expectations. Although difficult, this path can lead to legitimate success: a good college education, a well-paying job, material comfort, and often times praise from one's family and older (and fellow hard-working) community members.

The other path—what I refer to as *street life*—is more sexy. It is a downward slope, the gravity of neighborhood influence pulling in its direction. Prominent neighborhood "thugs" and "thuggish" role-models alike make it look easy and alluring. The majority of those who write about "street life" typically portray the lives of those dealing with homelessness. For the purposes of this book, street life denotes involvement in the criminal trades such as drug dealing, robbery, burglary, auto theft, prostitution, and smaller forms of street hustling.

Although intolerable to most in society, the path of street life promises wealth, a bounty of popularity and respect, and a chance at real power over nihilistic surroundings. Each choice can be made by all, but they are unequal in their availability, unfair in their distribution of accolades. For many young boys, the second path is the *only* choice; the first path, a poetic and unrealistic ideal. Often times one's community makes one choice more accessible than the other.

But within every dilapidated community, there are those conscientious entrepreneurs that attempt to create new opportunities for youth who face the crossroad. This book also explores the community-based programs that were cultivated to give crime-engaged youth a second chance. For decades, New York has been a leader in juvenile justice reform while simultaneously leading the country in greater punitive measures for adolescents. My focus on community-based programs is important, as *community justice* is a growing field of study and new frontier of practice.

In particular, I aim attention at *alternative-to-incarceration programs* as they are a newer form of juvenile justice sanctions and involve more community members. Alternative-to-incarceration programs (ATIs) for adolescents are literally an alternative to placement in prison, and they tend to be located within communities experiencing interruptions in public safety. They attempt to encourage community members' active involvement in the rehabilitation of its future adult members.

Juvenile crime in the United States reached its peak in the early 1990s and has been steadily declining ever since. As the 1990s progressed, drug use and violent crimes began to wane, but oddly enough, juvenile arrests were increasing: mostly new *status offenses* such as disorderly conduct, trespassing, running away from home, truancy, and loitering. The 1990s became a peak era in low tolerance to behaviors that many teens view as adventurous. By the end of the 1990s, juvenile incarceration rates were *increasing* leading to historic highs in prison populations. Juvenile detention has become the norm as more justice systems throughout the nation have adopted *adult waiver programs* which punish teenagers with adult sentences. Putting adolescents away for long periods of time can produce a battery of unintended consequences.

Imagine if you will, a fifteen-year-old boy who commits an act of premeditated armed robbery. A violent felony offense, this can earn the fifteen-year-old up to ten years in a New York state prison. Should this young person be tried as an adult? Your average person might say, "Absolutely, he needs to learn his lesson. Put him in for the max." We often forget to think about the future twenty-five-year-old and his imminent release from prison and reintegration into society. What can we expect from a twenty-five-year-old with no education, no job skills, and postponed social skills? Should we be surprised if he goes back to a criminal lifestyle within weeks of his release?

Urban adolescents in the poorest neighborhoods of America have been dealt a tough hand. As they mature, they often find themselves trapped in the lifeboat of post-industrial joblessness and panopticon-like neighborhood supervision. In urban ghettos, their survival—and their avoidance of the landmines set by the criminal justice system—must be preceded by knowledge of the materials available to them in their environment. If we are to expect adolescents to make good decisions and to survive in the post-industrial world without engagement in crime, then they have to be made aware of the opportunity structure available in their locality.

For youth who are not provided with conventional opportunities—or do not have access to these opportunities—they must be sought by unconventional means; in some cases, by means of deviant behavior; or in the case of alternative to incarceration programs, by innovative or improvised bridges to the necessary institutionalized means. As a response to the bankrupted opportunity structure left in urban ghettos, I claim that ATI programs attempt to provide a *social survival kit:* a set of tools designed for the successful navigation of a deprived environment.

The social survival kit is an emergency set of tools which attempt to address a dual set of circumstances confronting poor urban youth: 1) a global economy demanding that they take on more personal responsibility, and 2) a street culture that views hard work as slave labor. For the former, the consequences of not conforming to its norms are abject poverty or imprisonment; for the latter, the consequence is social isolation, a loss of neighborhood status, or possibly a violent end. Young boys in New York's most impoverished neighborhoods often live by a set of values that conflict with the legal codes. Successful survival in poor neighborhoods requires the acknowledgement of, and navigation through, the ever-present street life while simultaneously tip-toeing past the watching eye of the omnipresent criminal justice system. The task of the community-based ATI program is to prepare youths for both worlds.

The impossibility of this arduous path sparked my interest and led to years of research in New York's most deprived neighborhoods. Between 2004 and 2008, I spent hundreds of hours observing four private/non-profit ATI programs in New York City that serve Juvenile Offenders and Youthful Offenders. In each agency, there was an attempt to transfer a set of hard tools: computer skills, job training, anger management, for example; but this also tended to be coupled with a set of *soft tools*: motivation, conflict resolution skills, historical research skills, intellectual curiosity, and psychosocial empowerment. Once there was the recognition that *anomie* in some cases is a conditioned choice, then these agencies could build a set of tools for navigation on a practical and existentialist level.

The community organizations featured in this book dealt with the pitfalls of public education, faulty practices for the construction of social capital, reduced community involvement, along with the much ignored mental health and emotional issues that these kids deal with on a regular basis. The following chapters oscillate between the stories of crime-engaged youth in New York City and the community organizations that attempt to provide tools for leading a crime-free lifestyle. Chapter 1 explores juvenile justice in New York City, the world of ATI programs and the concept of community responsibility. Chapter 2 deals with the theoretical causes of the adolescent criminal behavior and the growing trend of diversion programs in the United States. Chapter 3 outlines the court process that is necessary for youth to have contact with ATI programs. Chapter 4 discusses the construction of masculinity in deprived neighborhoods and the magnetism of street life. Chapter 5 focuses on two programs: a Bronx-based ATI program and their direct use of community members as a means of building social capital, and a Manhattan-based program and their unique use of neighborhood residents as a model for community justice. Chapter 6 deals exclusively with a particular young man and the situation that led to his criminal endeavors. Chapter 7 profiles a "leadership training program" in Manhattan and its rigorous focus on *alternative education*; and a Brooklyn-based program and their adherence to the growing need for mental health services within the prison community. Chapter 8 discusses the role of teenagers in changing the juvenile justice policy that affects them. And chapter 9 is an empirical exploration of ATI programs and their sustainability in the current criminal justice system.

Chapter 1: Juvenile Justice and Community Responsibility

We are too accustomed to incarceration in the United States. The United States currently has a record number of inmates in jails and prisons (2.3 million and growing). There are also historically high numbers of incarcerated teenagers (over one hundred thousand[1]), mostly for what are categorized as misdemeanor or *status offenses* (i.e. petty larceny, disorderly conduct, or vandalism). Yet, policy makers do not see this as something that is urgent. If fact, many criminal justice officials would like to see these numbers *increase.*

Adolescents have come to symbolize what is dangerous in our society. Our youth are considered to be arrogant, impulsive, and unpredictable. As time goes on—and individual cases of teenage crime become more atrocious—some may find relief in knowing that more and more adolescent offenders are being punished like their adult counterparts. We feel safer knowing that the juvenile justice system is no longer "soft on crime." And just like the adult prison population, "bad" teens are removed from the community in the name of public safety.

According to the Citizens' Committee for Children of New York, Inc., juvenile arrests in New York City have increased 17 percent since 1996 even though adolescent involvement in felony crime has decreased 28 percent.[2] This is largely due to a 62 percent increase in misdemeanor arrests—a trend that has accelerated juvenile detention for crimes that previously led to minor Family Court supervision. More recently, juvenile *recidivism* rates in New York City[3] wildly exceed those of the adult prison population in the United States.[4] Two decades of annual increases in juvenile incarceration and the cost of imprisonment[5] have left many to seek new ways to improve public safety while simultaneously integrating its younger members back into society.

As a result, some are suggesting more radical changes to the juvenile justice system. Jeremy Travis—President of John Jay College of Criminal Justice—has even suggested that the tens of millions of dollars spent in poor New York neighborhoods for the supervision, arrests, and incarceration of neighborhood residents should be used for crime prevention and community development.[6] Many new scholars are exposing the deleterious effects of imprisoning fathers, wage-earners, and leaders of communities; but what about a community's *future*

Figure 1a: The "Deprived Dozen"

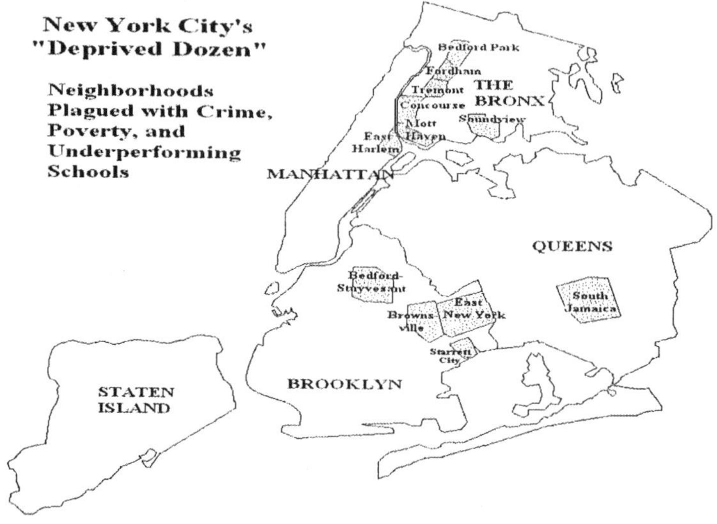

fathers, wage earners and leaders?

In New York City, the most common social characteristics of adolescent criminal offenders include being poor, being a person of color, living in an underperforming school district, and being part of a family whose adult members have extensive criminal histories. The combination of these traits is often an indication of *where* a person is from. Almost half of all of New York City's crime occurs in fifteen of its seventy-three police precincts. High crime tends to correlate with the *structural deprivation* that endures in certain parts of the city. Not to be confused with "cultural deprivation,"[7] structural deprivation denotes the impoverished institutionalized life chances that impede success in a social environment. When these life chances are deprived, so is the freedom of choice for youth in these environments.

As the nation's "safest big city"[8] is positioning itself to attract middle and upper income residents only, New York City government and business communities have noticeably by-passed the recovery of its working poor residents and instead have encouraged them to move out of the city as destitute neighborhoods dive *deeper* into social decay. This eventually allows for more rapid gentrification and urban renewal of forgotten communities. Poverty, crime, high unemployment, and underperforming schools tend to be concentrated into a select few New York neighborhoods, including: Starrett City, East New York, Soundview, Concourse, Mott Haven, Brownsville, Fordham, Tremont, Bedford Park, East Harlem, Bedford-Stuyvesant, and South Jamaica. For the sake of brevity, I will refer to this collection of neighborhoods from this point forward as the *deprived dozen.*[9]

Most of the neighborhoods that constitute the deprived dozen are either former industrial zones of New York City or immediately adjacent to these industrial zones. Even though it led the nation in F.I.R.E industries (Finance, Insurance, and Real Estate), by the mid-twentieth century New York City was a thriving industrial city that offered work for tens of thousands of low-skilled/uneducated workers. New York perfectly reflected Ernest Burgess' "Concentric Zone Model"[10] with its financial "loop" in downtown Manhattan; its factory zones in the Williamsburg, Long Island City, Port Morris, and Hunts Point neighborhoods in the outer boroughs; and its "working men's neighborhoods" of Bedford-Stuyvesant, Fort Greene, Woodside, and Mott Haven within walking distance of the factory zones.

Beginning in the 1960s, the combination of deindustrialization, "white flight," and a few controversial slum clearance initiatives[11] left many low-skilled persons of color to reinvent themselves in a changing city. Add the concentration of public housing to downward spiraling neighborhoods in Brooklyn and the Bronx, and this led to an increased descent of working class neighborhoods into ghetto oblivion. As was said by Janet Abu-Lughod in *New York, Chicago, Los Angeles* (1999), "confounding a simple model of 'white flight' . . . was the role that slum clearance and public housing played in changing the racial composition of Brooklyn [and the South Bronx]. . . . In the early 1940s and 1950s, large projects were built in Brownsville, Fort Greene, and Crown Heights, all districts into which the ghetto would expand."[12]

Neighborhoods that for decades provided working class stability—especially to African Americans in the 1940s and Puerto Ricans in the 1960s—rapidly became zones barren of commercial enterprise and full of hopelessly unemployed residents. By the beginning of the 1970s, crime rates in New York City (and nationwide) began to trend upward. The 1970s, in particular, created the template for the structural deprivation that still persists today. A bankrupt New York City, a national economy in recession, and a failing job market hit New York's deprived dozen the hardest. President Jimmy Carter's famous visit to the South Bronx in 1977 put a spotlight on the rapid deterioration of a former industrial zone. As he drove through, people could be heard screaming, "Give us money!" and "We want jobs!"[13] Even though he was said to have seen the "devastation" first hand, little was done to reverse the trend.

Three decades later, New York City still has very little to offer for low-skilled/uneducated workers. According to the New York City Department of City Planning, the city experienced a 26.6 percent decrease in manufacturing between 2001 and 2005 alone. "In 2005, private employment was predominantly distributed in health care and social assistance (18 percent), finance and insurance (11 percent); professional and technical services (10 percent); and retail trade (9 percent) sectors."[14] All but the retail sector require college-level education or years of vocational training. The Bronx and Brooklyn are trending in this direction the most, as most of the industrial sites have been converted for use by the warehousing industries (a 23 percent increase from 2001 to 2005).

Today, New York ranks thirteenth in major U.S. cities with children living below the poverty line (27.4 percent). 65.5 percent of its African American children and 71 percent of Latino children are born into poverty in each year.[15] The negative conditions propounded on New York City's former working class neighborhoods have created an acknowledged cultural expectation of criminal deviance; what Loic Wacquant (1999) has called "the regime of urban marginality." Urban youth, in particular, are lining up to join the ranks of the *hustler class* which consequently and effortlessly provides fodder for the criminal justice system. As was said best by Wacquant:

> Post-industrial modernization translates, on the one hand, into the multiplication of highly skilled positions for university-trained professional and technical staff and, on the other, into the deskilling and outright elimination of millions of jobs for uneducated workers. . . . A significant fraction of the working class has been rendered redundant and composes an *absolute surplus population* that will probably never find regular work again.[16]

A select few of the lower economic stratum will be able to bridge the gap to monetary success with a good education, support from family, and well-placed social capital inside the job market. Others will choose the more widely available march into the criminal trades.

The normalization of illicit economic activity in the deprived dozen has been the typical response to joblessness in former working class areas. As Robert Merton (1996) would argue, "the consequence of this structural inconsistency is a comparative high rate of deviant behavior."[17] Take, for example, the undeniable correlation between neighborhoods with high poverty rates and the number of "financial crimes" in the same neighborhoods. (See figure 1b.)

As the youth of New York City begin to come of age, it is important for them to flesh out what is necessary for social mobility in a post-industrial urban society. If we expect teenagers to stay away from the hustlers' economy and become productive members of society, they need a precise set of skills in order to achieve legitimate financial freedom. Included should be a quality post-secondary education, good health and safe environment, strong literacy and technological skills, a strong work ethic, and (because of shrinking demand and growing competition in the professional world) good social connections within the job market. Youth who live in New York's deprived dozen are already born with several strikes against them; and some will never have access to any of these necessary resources.

For New York's adolescent population, the future offers little promise if they are to conform to contemporary institutionalized opportunities. Current economic forces drive youth to two choices: (a) towards an extremely finite legitimate path to join the increasing army of working poor in the services economy; or (b) to the more attractive illegitimate path of *street life*. Although street life involves criminal activity, it also promises *fast money* and highly popular cultural status. Many of the crimes committed by young people tend be crimes relative

Figure 1b: Household Income in New York City Compared to Number of Robberies

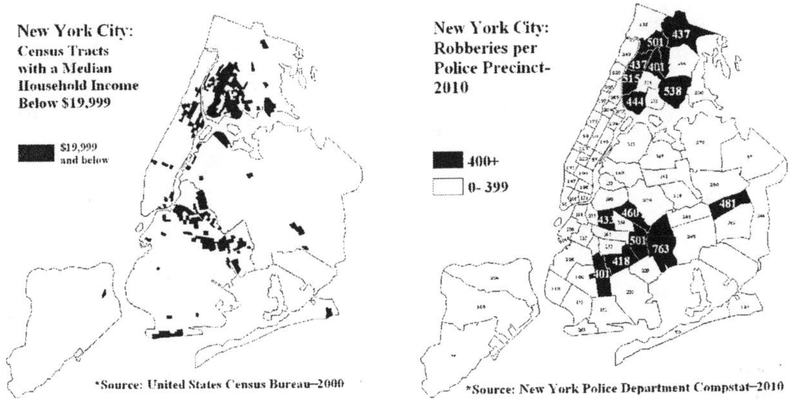

to the accumulation of money, such as theft, robbery, or the sale of illegal drugs. According to the NYPD, larceny theft is the biggest of all crimes in the city.

Not all of New York's teen population is destined to fall into the ranks of the absolute surplus, but a particular few who have been subject to New York's deprived conditions will transition more easily into New York's criminal justice system. If the "prison industrial complex"[18] (suggesting that prisons manufacture wealth for certain segments of the market economy) is real and tangible, then New York's deprived dozen is the assembly line for the manufacturing of criminals.

Youth who are subject to the aforementioned adverse social conditions will likely be "differentially exposed to criminal behavior patterns"[19] compared to their peers in higher economic stratums. As a result, involvement in the criminal trades has more meaning to a young person with fewer meaningful choices. As juvenile crime rates abound in New York's deprived dozen, many outside *and* inside of these communities favor current policies that lock away wayward youth until they reach full physical maturity. If it is true—as the old proverb claims—that "it takes a village to raise a child," then the construction of community needs to take into consideration its younger members. Like most other social problems, we look to our criminal justice system to maintain social control over our youngest members. Community members typically look at other people's children simply as *other people's children.* Responsibility falls on the parent, and sometimes goes a notch below to that of the state. The movement to take young neighborhood residents out of the hands of the community and into the hands of the state is, historically speaking, new. The juvenile justice system has waxed and waned between total community involvement and disengagement, which has a strong correlation to the rise and fall of juvenile crime over the past century.

Criminalization of Juvenile Delinquency

Public safety is inherently a perception—a perception that often demands concrete results. Over the past three decades, politicians and criminal justice officials have operated under the assumption that increased criminalization of deviant behavior will lead to increased public safety: with more criminals in prison, they are less likely to cause additional harm. Of course, the biggest "kink" in this chain of thought is that 95 percent of incarcerated offenders are eventually released back to their respective communities. But for better or worse, the "modus operandi" in New York is to remain "tough on crime."

Since the 1980s, the New York City Police Department has wholly adopted the ideal of punishing deviant behavior in order to prevent more serious crimes from occurring. This ideal is reflected in James Wilson and George Kelling's (1982) now famous "broken windows theory." They suggest that small, non-criminal deviant acts should be criminalized because "untended behavior also leads to the breakdown of community controls."[20] Of course, this inevitably leads to increased incarceration of non-violent offenders, but the community feels safer.

For the perceived normalization of criminal behavior amongst adolescents, the official response has been to choose more punitive methods for dealing with this behavior, including: increasing arrests and sentencing; criminalizing more disorderly behavior; and incarcerating more anti-social youth than ever before in our history. The move to criminalize delinquency has been popularized by its perceived guarantee of public safety. This development is contrary to the original intentions of the juvenile justice system in New York which was designed to "reform juveniles and prevent future criminal behavior."[21]

By design, the adult criminal justice system and juvenile justice system are designed to operate on different model types. As is said by Aaron Kupchik in *Judging Juveniles* (2006), "Relative to a juvenile justice model, the criminal justice model suggests that the processing is formal, evaluation of offenders is centered on offense-relevant criteria rather than offender-relevant criteria, and the primary goals of sentencing are to punish and deter rather than rehabilitate."[22] The juvenile justice model, on the other hand, was designed to examine the individual offender in order to forge a path to rehabilitation.

As far back as the 1820s, neo-classical thinkers conceded that children did not possess the capacity to determine right from wrong, and therefore, could not be held fully accountable for their criminal behavior. Juvenile detention centers were places for education rather than punishment. This era in juvenile justice would later be named the "Child Saving Movement" which produced reformers such as Stephen Allen, Charles Loring Brace and Jane Addams. For more than 150 years, juvenile justice adopted the role of *parens patriae* (parent of the country): picking up the educational slack where schools and families had failed. With the creation of the Illinois Juvenile Court Act of 1899—the first juvenile court in the country—Justice Julian Mack was quoted as saying, "Why is it not the duty of the state . . . not to make him a criminal, but a worthy citizen."[23]

What collated into the juvenile justice system by the early twentieth century was focused more so on the interests of the child than any push for retribution. The opening of the New York House of Refuge—the first juvenile detention facility in the United States—would serve as the model for educating adolescent offenders and guiding them towards productive citizenship. Of course, many criticized the Child-Saving Movement for imposing middle class values on poor children and neglecting the concerns of the parents. As was said by Anthony Platt in *Child Savers* (1969) "The use of terms like 'unsocialized,' 'maladjusted,' and 'pathological,' to describe the behavior of delinquents implied that 'socialized' and 'adjusted' children conform to middle-class morality and participate in respectable institutions."[24]

Nonetheless, by the mid-twentieth century, much of this energy began to spill into all areas of the criminal justice system. The reformatory nature of the juvenile justice system would later be renamed the "medical model" in order to fit the adult system. This model was focused on the criminal offender as a patient: someone who could be treated and cured of their criminal impulses. By the 1950s, the adult criminal justice system adopted these ideals by imposing indeterminate sentences on adult offenders and focusing on treatment before prisoner release. In 1944, California Governor (and future Supreme Court Justice) Earl Warren "authorized the construction of specialized prisons and the creation of the California Adult Authority. [This new system] developed a full range of treatment programs, including psychotherapy and group therapy."[25]

Nationwide, prisons were renamed "correctional facilities"; prison guards became "corrections officers"; and offender rehabilitation became the top priority. Much like the classical thinkers of prison reform—such as Jeremy Bentham—correctional facilities became places where prisoners could be "observed and instructed"[26] to live more productive/crime-free lives. For a small moment in the early 1960s, both juvenile justice and criminal justice models focused on rehabilitation, and it can be argued that these systems were married from that point forward—both relying heavily on the medical model, and then rapidly moving away from it.

With a changing political climate and rising crime rates in the late 1960s, many deemed the medical model to be a failure, and the adult criminal justice system moved back towards punishment and deterrence as their major modes. The juvenile justice system in New York made a simultaneous turn with the Family Court Act of 1962, which gave adolescent offenders due process rights. Although this gave juveniles the right to the administration of law (as afforded in the adult system), this also took away the court's ability to judge a young person by their character and instead solely on the circumstances of the crime.

Under the Nixon and Ford Administrations in the 1970s, increased punishments became the norm for both the adult and juvenile systems. New York State always seemed to lead the charge that the rest of the country would follow. New York's Juvenile Justice Reform Act of 1976 required Family Court to "consider the community's need for protection as well as the needs and the best interests of the child."[27] This act was the first of its kind, making the concerns of the community co-equals with that of the child and the child's family. What is implied is the child's potential danger to a community, and now judges can introduce more "restrictive placement" for designated felony offenses. By 1978—with a few small adjustments to the Juvenile Justice Reform Amendment—adolescents could serve hard time for murder, robbery, rape, burglary and assault.

With increasing structural deprivation in New York City in the 1970s, and subsequent ascending crimes rates, there was a pressure build leading up to the summer of 1978. The largest change to juvenile justice policy in New York was inspired by one young boy: Willie Bosket, Jr. Between March 19 and March 27, 1978, fifteen-year-old Willie Bosket murdered two men with an illegal firearm. New York State law at the time could only give him a maximum of five years imprisonment. Some assumed this was a scared little boy possibly firing out of fear or self-defense, but as the story began to reveal itself it was found that Willie enjoyed what he had done, even "giggling" over it when he read about it in the morning paper the next day.[28]

Community residents in the New York began to cry foul. Mayor Koch called him a "mad dog killer." People wanted justice, so the New York legislature sprung into action over the summer. New York Governor Hugh Carey—who had been considered soft on crime up to that point—completely changed his stance. The *New York Times* was quoted as saying, "The day after the Bosket youth's five year sentence was announced, the governor said for the first time that he would support giving prosecutors the discretion to try juveniles in adult courts."[29] On September 1, 1978 the Juvenile Offender Law was created as part of the Omnibus Crime Control Bill. This law essentially merged the juvenile justice and adult systems in the instance of felony crime.

The Juvenile Offender Law (or "J.O. Law") "created a new class of defendant called the 'Juvenile Offender' to whom the statutory defense of infancy against criminal charges was no longer available."[30] Juveniles were now deemed fully responsible for felony acts. Prior to that, defense attorneys could use the "infancy defense" for anyone under sixteen arguing that their client did not know the difference between right and wrong.

This began the move towards what Simon Singer (2003) calls the *recriminalization of delinquency*. "By diverting the most difficult and violent of juveniles away from the juvenile justice system, the recriminalization of delinquency attempts to satisfy public and official demands to see serious delinquents punished in public, criminal court." [31] The "J.O. law" created new standards for determining the severity of juvenile crimes, the imposition of adult punishments for juvenile offenders, two new categories for adolescent offenders,[32] and the practice of waiving the right of juveniles to attend juvenile courts. (See figure 1c.)

After 1978, forty-eight other states and the federal government followed New York's lead by creating their own "waiver laws." As a part of the federal Comprehensive Crime Control Act of 1984, more punitive measures were instilled for juveniles who violated federal law. As was said by Aaron McNeece &

Table 1c: Juvenile Offender Law Sentencing Procedures

Class A Offense	**Minimum**	**Maximum**
Murder 2	5-9 years[33]	Life
Arson 1	4-6 years	12-15 years
Kidnapping 1		
Class B Offense	**Minimum**	**Maximum**
Manslaughter 1	1-3 years	3-10 years
Rape; Robbery 1		
Burglary 1; Arson 2		
Sodomy 1; Attempted Murder 1		
Aggravated Sexual Abuse		
Attempted Kidnapping 1		
Class C Offense	**Minimum**	**Maximum**
Burglary 2	up to1-2 years	3-7 years
Robbery 2		
Assault 1		
Class C Offense	**Minimum**	**Maximum**
Crim. Poss. of a Weapon	up to1-2 years	3-4 years

Sherry Jackson in their article *Juvenile Justice Policy: Current Trends and 21st Century Issues* (2004) "The Reagan Administration believed that for too long the juvenile justice system had been overly concerned with the protection of juvenile offenders at the expense of society and it victims."[34]

In recent years, adolescents have been portrayed in the media as "super-predators"[35] with uncontrollably violent urges only to be absolved through incarceration. And as juvenile crime peaked in the early 1990s, so did the legal response to it. "Between 1992 and 1997, forty-five states modified state laws and juvenile procedures in order to make their juvenile justice systems more punitive."[36]

Nationwide, juvenile crime has been trending downward since 1993, and many would claim it is because of these measures. Yet most of the crimes that adolescents are being arrested for are not typically attached to public fear of crime. According to the U.S. Department of Justice, there are over two million juvenile arrests each year; most commonly for larceny theft (15.3 percent of all juvenile arrests), disorderly conduct (8.9 percent), drug abuse (8.5 percent), and loitering or curfew violations (6.3 percent).[37] Although juvenile crime rates are significantly lower than adults', new policies—combined with public perception—have allowed juvenile detention in New York City to increase at a 6 percent annual rate. Juveniles commit about 16 percent of total crimes in the United

States, yet media coverage makes them out to be the largest crime problem in America. What is more disturbing is that incarceration alone does not seem to be much of a deterrent to crime.

A 2009 report composed by the New York State Office of Children and Family Services discovered that "offense history, childhood maltreatment, prior receipt of child welfare services, and family environment were associated with heightened risk for adult antisocial behavior for both boys and girls."[38] In this study of juvenile crime in New York State, 85 percent of boys and 68 percent of girls were convicted of new crimes after serving time in New York's prison system. Although they may be more "cozy" than adult prisons, juvenile detention centers are designed to manufacture law-abiding citizens and scare children out of ever returning; but the latest research suggests that confinement alone increases the chances of continued criminal behavior.

There is a movement in its infancy in New York's juvenile justice system that recognizes the deficiencies of prisons for crime prevention, and is making adjustments accordingly. The New York City Department of Juvenile Justice (DJJ) is beginning a re-facing by merging its juvenile detention services with the Administration for Children's Services (a branch of city government that typically deals with child welfare and abuse). In a July 2010 public statement, DJJ claimed that "there is a widespread agreement among all stakeholders that there should be intensive, evidence-based services available to this population and that certain youth charged as juvenile offenders could be safely maintained in the community."[39] State, city, and non-profit agencies alike are slowly reconsidering more rehabilitative efforts after three decades of harsh punitive tactics; and they are now looking to community-based alternative-to-incarceration programs as a viable option.

Alternative-to-Incarceration Programs as Community Responsibility

Alternative-to-incarceration programs (ATIs) in New York City were created to fulfill a certain set of needs lacking in the current juvenile justice system: not only to provide a substitute for incarceration, but to create viable opportunities for youth who have violated the legal codes. Prisons and jails were designed to operate outside of the community; to be separate from society. But even after their return to the community, we now know that former inmates remain outside of the structure of society. Grassroots community-based organizations are now attempting to provide young people with the proper tools to survive as *post-industrial utilitarians*.

For many of us, *a social survival kit* comes from good family, good schooling, and good community. For the underprivileged youth of the deprived dozen, survival and success—without involvement in the criminal trades—requires additional cultural assistance. Sociologist Ann Swidler (1986) spoke of culture as a "tool kit of symbols, stories, rituals, world views" which can then be used for "strategies of action."[40] All individuals in society gather a tool kit from their cultures for meaningful induction into the world stage. A social survival kit—a necessary addendum in disadvantaged communities—provides the transference of tools displaced by traditional social institutions. Whereas many children will learn about financial responsibility by watching their parents pay bills, other will learn by watching the hustlers on the corner.

ATIs in New York City are reflections of the Child Saving Movement as they seek to create "good citizens" while allowing juveniles to stay in their own communities. Yet today's ATIs are being constructed in deprived communities, and unlike Child Saving organizations of the past, are using the resources available to them from working poor residents. One could argue that stalwarts such as Jane Addams and Loring Brace were imposing misguided middle class values on poor kids. Brace's "Children's Aid Society" permanently removed poor children from their families in the late nineteenth century and "farmed" them in wealthy homes. It was thought that it was too late for the adult members of poor communities. The original Child Saving Movement "was based on the assumption that proper training can counteract the impositions of poor family life, a corrupt environment, and poverty, while at the same time toughening and preparing delinquents for the struggle ahead."[41] Modern ATIs make use of all its community members.

Of course, not all ATIs nationwide are designed to serve youth. State and municipal criminal justice agencies typically use the following as alternatives to imprisonment: a) probation, b) boot camps, c) home detention, d) electronic monitoring, e) intensive probation monitoring, f) day reporting, g) community service, and h) "inpatient" treatment programs.[42] Probation alone monitors close to 4.1 million adjudicated offenders nationwide.

Together, these approaches are viewed as a form of community justice. Many have argued that the "prison experiment" is failing, and therefore, the criminal justice system is seeking alternatives. According to the U.S. Department of Justice, 67.5 percent of prisoners released from state custody will be rearrested within three years (80 percent for men alone).[43] As a result, there are more people being monitored by the state than are incarcerated, and individuals monitored in their own communities are producing lower recidivism rates.

Municipal judicial branches have gotten in on the act with the creation of *crime-specific courts* including: drug abuse courts in New York City; mental health courts in Denver, Colorado; veterans' courts in Nevada and Illinois; and sex worker courts in Franklin County, Ohio. Small reforms have been made to reduce the prison population, therefore, more courts are choosing the medical model over what appears to be ineffective punitive strategies. This has opened the door for smaller non-profit ATIs to provide services to criminal offenders.

Around New York City, there are many adult programs for offenses that demand treatment, such as drug abuse, prostitution, and mental health services. City and state officials have been slow to warm up to programs that offer a chance at reformation for violent offenders, but there is a small contingent that is willing to give adolescents additional opportunities.

A small percentage of youth indicted in New York City are given a chance to participate in one of the city's community-based ATI programs. These youth-oriented ATIs focus on rehabilitating youth post-adjudication, typically before a youth has been sentenced. Many court judges look at these community-based programs as a second chance for youth who may otherwise never recover from the stigma of a criminal record. ATI programs are said to be more successful at rehabilitating youth and training them to lead a crime-free lifestyle as they approach adulthood.

The New York State Office of Probation and Correctional Alternatives (OPCA) funds over 165 ATI programs statewide. They generally target mental illness, pretrial services, drug and alcohol addiction, and community service. These programs are expanding—some with a focus on public safety—others with a focus on rebuilding community relations.

For the services of juvenile delinquents, juvenile offenders and youthful offenders, there are eight major players in New York City, including: 1) The Court Employment Project (created by the Center for Alternative Sentencing and Employment Services); 2) The Dome Project's Juvenile Justice Program; 3) The Youth Advocacy Project (created by the Center for Community Alternatives, Inc.); 4) The Andrew Glover Youth Program; 5) The Kings County Juvenile Offender Program (under the New York City Department of Probation); 6) Assigned Counsel Services (created by the Osborne Association); 7) The Bronx-Connect Youth Program (created by the Urban Youth Alliance, International); and 8) The Staten Island TASC Adolescent Diversion Program (under the Educational and Assistance Corporation). Many of these programs are funded by the New York State Division of Probation and Correctional Alternatives, while others pool their money from private donors.

A handful of research and news organizations have featured reports on some of these organizations, but none have been inside to view the inner workings of these initiatives. None have explored *how* they function; *how* they deliver their services. A large paradigmatic puzzle in criminology is whether rehabilitative services are even useful. *Do they* increase public safety? Or are there just to satisfy the desires of "bleeding-heart liberals" who want to wish society's crime problem away? It was James Q. Wilson who—at the beginning of the "tough on crime" transformation of the 1970s—said that "rehabilitation has not yet been shown to be a promising method for dealing with serious offenders" and that "deterrence and incapacitation work."[44]

Around the same time, Robert Martinsen's (1974) politically charged study of 231 rehabilitative programs in the United States resulted in him saying that there is "no appreciable effect—positive or negative—on rates of recidivism."[45] This created a well regarded sentiment that "nothing works," and punitive methods are the only solution to crime. Since then little effort has been put into the exploration of ATI programs, as few are taken seriously by many criminologists. Here was the hole in my literature review and an opportunity to create a new research endeavor.

Here was the hole in my literature review and an opportunity to create a new research endeavor.

Between January 2004 and December 2006, I engaged in an ethnographic exploration of four ATI programs. I originally intended to do research inside all eight of the big ATI programs in New York City, but many were resistant to the eyes of an outsider. I observed that the programs with the greatest amount of city or state funding were concerned with the "legal complications" my research could create, therefore, I was denied access. As a result, I was able to gain access to the programs which depended more on private sources. This included the BronxConnect Youth Program (located in Mott Haven neighborhood of the Bronx); the Andrew Glover Youth Program (located in the Lower East Side of Manhattan), and Brooklyn Adolescent Link (located in Brooklyn Heights); and the Each One Teach One Youth Leadership Training Program (at the time, located in the Greenwich Village neighborhood of Manhattan).[46] By embedding myself in these programs, and through numerous interviews with program directors, staff and participants, I gained access to the world of alternative sanctions for adolescents. Each program included services typically not found inside of secure detention, including: anger management courses, job training, legal rights counseling, individual therapy, family counseling, and outpatient mental health treatment referrals. (See table 1d.)

The BronxConnect Youth Program employed what I call the *community circuit model.* BronxConnect served court-involved youth between the ages of thirteen and eighteen. Located in one of the poorest neighborhoods in New York City, the program pooled social capital from its most successful community members. BronxConnect utilized adult mentors from the community in order to educate and guide their adolescent clients. By serving as positive examples for the youth, the adult mentors established real connections and potential opportunities in one of the city's most deprived neighborhoods. The program also networked with other agencies in the community, reestablishing fading community ties.

The Andrew Glover Youth Program made use of what I call the *total community justice model.* In this model, the program's staff, clients and guest speakers all came from the Lower East Side of Manhattan. By taking actual community members and charging them to work with court-involved youth, they were doubly invested in the success of the adolescents and neighborhood safety. Andrew Glover had two sites, one in the Lower East Side one in East Harlem—each relying solely on its own community members for supervision.

The Brooklyn Adolescent Link Program employed the *mental health institutional nexus model.* Whereas, BronxConnect and Andrew Glover were like day-reporting centers (requiring their clients to be involved in daily on-site activities), Brooklyn Adolescent Link served as a hub for mental health outsourcing. This program only worked with court-involved youth with some sort of diagnosable mental or behavioral disorder.[47] Clients were not required to report to the program for activities, but instead would be referred to the numerous amounts of inpatient and outpatient mental health treatment facilities scattered

Table 1d: Four Youth ATI Programs and the Ingredients for a Survival Kit

Each One TeachOne	BronxConnect	Andrew Glover	Brooklyn Link
*Alternative Education	*Case Management	*Case Management	*Case Management
*Conflict Resolution	*Court Advocacy	*Court Advocacy	*Court Advocacy
*Internship Program	*Mentoring	*Community Membership	*Individual Counseling
*Legal Rights Course	*Faith-Based Counseling	*Job Training	*Mental Health Services
*History Training	*Anger Management	*Health & Sex Education	*Health Service Referrals
*Advocacy Training	*Job Training	*Arts and Games	*Substance Abuse
*Cultural Exploration	*Conflict Resolution	*Life Skills Training	*Residential Treatment

throughout New York City. Brooklyn Adolescent Link is no longer operational today because funding streams have been directed towards their adult programs.

The Each One Teach One Youth Leadership Training was different in that it was not tied to any court mandates, but by design, 50 percent of its participants were court-involved youth. Founded under the Correctional Association of New York, this program employed what I call the *cultural empowerment model.* Participants ages thirteen to seventeen volunteered to be a part of the training which focused on African American and Latino history, legal rights in New York City, and the pressures of dealing with deprived neighborhood conditions.

With the permission of the program directors, I was able to embed myself in these programs as either a "mentor," a "volunteer," or an "assistant group facilitator." All program staff and court-involved participants were made fully aware of my presence and research intentions. Throughout the two years of qualitative research, I combined both participant observation with qualitative interviewing. Most of programs met twice weekly at night where they would engage in program activities. Sometimes I would show up early to interview staff and participants, and on other occasions, I would be involved in the activities themselves.

Youth in BronxConnect, Andrew Glover, and Brooklyn Adolescent Link were obligated to receive services from the programs as part of a *conditional release* to their communities. The programs ran anywhere from twelve to eighteen month cycles, therefore, I would enter at the beginning of a cycle and observe their techniques in action. The Each One Teach One program ran in six month training cycles. I would generally spend one evening at each program per week, (except for Brooklyn Adolescent Link because they only provided one-on-one sessions with their case managers). The activities consisted of *life skills* sessions or group activities, in which I would participate in solely as a facilitator of planned questions, activities, or round-table discussions. Most of these activities would take place after school hours for up to three hours at a time (typically 5pm-8pm) on-site. In some cases, court mandates required daily attendance, while others required only one visit per week.

After two years of ethnographic research, other questions began to surface. How effective are these programs at reducing recidivism? Did successful completion of these programs translate to a crime-free lifestyle and improved quality of life for former participants? All of the programs claimed to be successful at reducing recidivism rates, but none had the empirical evidence to support it. Thus began the second leg of my research.

Between December 2007 and December 2008, I set out to follow up with some of the former clients of BronxConnect and the Each One Teach One program. I made an arrangement with the New York State Division of Criminal Justice Services (DCJS) to look over the criminal histories of nearly three hundred former ATI clients. Like the first leg of my research, I solicited the top eight youth ATI programs, but I was met with some resistance because of fear of the results.

I also added a qualitative component to the second leg of the research by tracking down and interviewing former clients of BronxConnect, Brooklyn Adolescent Link, and Each One Teach One. This also required permission of the program directors. The following chapters represent the results of both legs of this research. All of the youth's names were changed for anonymity, but program staff, directors and criminal justice officials' names were kept intact after gaining their permission to do so.

Youth ATI programs had to address both the structural deprivation that exists in New York City and the magnetism of criminal street culture that endures in the deprived dozen. Small community-based programs may represent the future of juvenile justice reform, as they actively involve those with the most to lose (and to gain) if adolescents cannot be shown the path to crime-free post-industrial utilitarianism. Community members are up against structural, as well as cultural forces, that often lead adolescents to the slippery slope of deviant behavior, therefore, only a precise set of tools can ever be effective.

Notes

1. Snyder, Howard and Melissa Sickmund. *Juvenile Offenders and Victims: 2006 National Report.* Washington, D.C.: Office of Juvenile Justice and Delinquency Prevention, 2006.

2. Scheer, Rebecca. "Keeping Track of New York City Children: A Status Report 2010." A Citizens' Committee for Children of New York, Inc., 2010.

3. If recidivism is measured in new arrests after serving time in prison, 89 percent of boys and 81 percent girls eventually recidivate in New York. If measured in new convictions, 85 percent of boys and 68 percent of girls recidivate in New York.

4. Coleman, Rebecca, Susan Mitchel-Herzfeld, Do Han Kim, and Therese A. Shady. "Long-Term Consequences of Delinquency: Child Maltreatment and Crime in Early Adulthood." *Final Report.* (U.S. Department of Justice: National Institute of Justice, March 31, 2009).

5. According to New York State Executive Budget Documents (2007-2008), New York State spends $150 million per year to incarcerate youth in juvenile institutions.

6. Travis, Jeremy. *But They All Come Back: Facing the Challenges of Reentry.* Washington, D.C.: The Urban Institute Press, 2005.

7. Arthur Pearl. "Cultural and Accumulated Environmental Deficit Models." Richard Valencia [Ed.] *The Evolution of Deficit Thinking: Educational Thought and Practice.* Bristol, Penn. Falmers Press, 1997.

8. New York City Government. "Making the Nation's Safest Big City Even Safer." Retrieved July 19, 2010 from New York City government website: http://home2.nyc.gov/html/dot/downloads/pdf/stratplan_safety.pdf.

9. Deprived Dozen determined by creating a "deprivation score" = median household income (divided by 100) – total violent crime (times .258) – average standardized test score per school district. Lower score means worse deprivation.

10. Park, Robert E. & Ernest Burgess. *The City.* Chicago, IL: University of Chicago Press, 1925.

11. The construction of the Cross Bronx Expressway, in particular, was said to displace over 170,000 residents in the South Bronx between 1948 and 1972.

12. Abu-Lughod, Janet. *New York, Chicago, Los Angeles: America's Global Cities.* Minneapolis: University of Minnesota Press, 1999.

13. Dembart, Lee. (October 6, 1977). "Carter Takes Sobering Trip to South Bronx." *New York Times.* P. A66.

14. Burden, Amanda. "Social Indicators." *City of New York Department of City Planning 2005 Annual Report.*

15. Rebecca Scheer, p. 20.

16. Wacquant, Loic (1999). "Urban Marginality in the Coming Millenium." *Urban Studies*, Vol. 36 (10), 1639-1647.

17. Merton, Robert K. "Social Structure and Anomie." *On Social Structure and Science.* Chicago, Ill.: University of Chicago Press, 1996.

18. Davis, A. (Sept. 1998). "Masked Racism: Reflections on the Prison Industrial Complex." *Color Lines.* p. A1.

19. Sutherland, Edwin and Donald Cressey. *Principles of Criminology.* Lanham, Md.: AltaMira Press, 1939.

20. Wilson, James and George Kelling. "Broken Windows." *The Atlantic Monthly.* March 1982, pp. 29-38.

21. Robert Mennel. "Origins of the Juvenile Court." Thomas Calhoun and Constance L. Chapple [Eds.] *Readings in Juvenile Delinquency and Juvenile Justice. 3rd Ed.* Upper Saddle River, N.J.: Pearson Education, 2003.

22. Kupchik, Aaron. *Judging Juveniles: Prosecuting Adolescents in Juvenile and Adult Courts.* New York: New York University Press, 2006.

23. Robert Mennel, p. 80.

24. Platt, Anthony. *The Child Savers.* Chicago, Ill.: University of Chicago Press, 1969.

25. Clear, Todd R., George F. Cole, and Michael Reisig. *American Corrections* (8th edition). Belmont, Calif.: Thomson Wadsworth, 2009.

26. Bentham, Jeremy. *The Panopticon Writings.* Verso Books, 1995.

27. Warner, Eric. *The Juvenile Offender Handbook: A Comprehensive Guide to the "J.O. Law" and Related Statutes.* New York: Looseleaf Publications, 2007.

28. Butterfield, Fox. *All God's Children: The Bosket Family and the American Tradition of Violence.* New York: Harper Collins, 1995.

29. Kaiser, C. (July 20, 1978). "Youth Held in 2 Murders Asked for Placement in Foster Home." *The New York Times,* p. B2.

30. Warner, Eric. *The Juvenile Offender Handbook: A Comprehensive Guide to the "J.O. Law" and Related Statutes.* p. 4.

31. Singer, Simon. *Recriminalizing Delinquency: Violent Juvenile Crime & Juvenile Justice Reform.* New York: Cambridge University Press, 1996.

32. 1. *Juvenile Delinquent,* (defined in Family Court Act 1962) a person at least seven years old and younger than sixteen who commits an act which would be a crime if committed by an adult, but whose conduct is not criminal.

2. *Juvenile Offender,* (defined in J.O. law 1978) a person thirteen, fourteen, or fifteen years old who is deemed criminally responsible for specific acts because such acts are excluded from the statutory defense of infancy. AND a thirteen-year-old is criminally responsible only for acts constituting murder in the second degree.

3. *Youthful Offender,* (not specifically defined by law) Y.O. status is typically provided to first time or non-felony offenders ages 16 and 17.

33. Minimum sentence increased to seven and a half to fifteen years for fourteen and fifteen-year-olds convicted of intentional or "depraved indifference" murder.

34. McNeece, C. Aaron and Sherry Jackson. "Juvenile Justice Policy: Current Trends and 21st Century Issues." *Juvenile Justice Sourcebook: Past, Present and Future.* New York: Oxford University Press, 2004.

35. DiIulio, John. *Body Count: Moral Poverty and How to Win America's War Against Crime and Drugs.* New York: Simon and Schuster, 1996.

36. Roberts, Albert R. *Juvenile Justice Sourcebook: Past, Present and Future.* New York: Oxford University Press, 2004.

37. Puzzanchere, Charles. "Juvenile Arrests 2008." *Juvenile Justice Bulletin* (U.S. Department of Justice: Office of Juvenile Prevention, Dec. 2009).

38. Coleman, Rebecca, Do Han Kim, Susan Mitchell-Herzfeld, and Therese Shady. "Long-Term Consequences of Delinquency: Child Maltreatment and Crime in Early Adulthood." (Report by the New York State Office of Children and Family Services-March 31, 2009).

39. New York City Department of Juvenile Justice. "Building On Success: Next Steps in New York City Detention Reform." Retrieved on July 21, 2010 from http://www.nyc.gov/html/djj/pdf/detention_reform_action_plan.pdf.

40. Swidler, Ann (April 1986). "Culture in Action: Symbols and Strategies." *American Sociological Review* (51), pp. 273-286.

41. Anthony Platt. "The Rise of the Child-Saving Movement." *Readings in Juvenile Delinquency and Juvenile Justice. 3rd Ed.*(Upper Saddle River, N.J.: Pearson Education, 2003).

42. Austin, James, Kelly Johnson, and Ronald Weitzer. "Alternatives to Secure Detention and Confinement of Juvenile Offenders." Retrieved July 30, 2010 from U.S. Department of Justice's Office of Juvenile Justice and Delinquency Prevention website: http://www.ncjrs.gov/pdffiles1/ojjdp/208804.pdf.

43. Bureau of Justice Statistics. "Recidivism in the United States." U.S. Department of Justice, 2009.

44. Wilson, James Q. *Thinking About Crime.* New York: Basic Books, 1983.

45. Martinson, R. (Spring 1974). "What Works?: Questions and Answers About Prison Reform," *The Public Interest*, pp. 22-54.

46. The Each One Teach One Youth Leadership Training Program is technically not an ATI program, but provides similar services to at-risk youth.

47. Adolescents with a diagnosable mental illness are labeled as having "serious emotional disturbance" by New York State.

Chapter 2: Adolescent Criminal Behavior and the Use of Diversion Programs

Before I was an ethnographer or college professor, I was a court advocate for a Brooklyn-based alternative-to-incarceration program. My job was to provide progress reports to the Criminal and Supreme Court systems. I traveled between Brooklyn, Manhattan and the Bronx, as this was where the program pooled its clients from. I would typically advocate for the conditional release of adolescent criminal offenders, and then report back to the courts within a few weeks.

On one particular occasion, I had just left Brooklyn Supreme Court with a sixteen-year-old boy named Dominic. The youth part judge had just released Dominic from a thirty-day *remand* (preventative detention) after violating some of the conditions of his original release, and I was ordered by the judge to personally escort him to his mother's apartment in Coney Island, Brooklyn.

Dominic was big for his age, maybe six-foot-three and weighing over two hundred pounds. His green eyes lit up as he watched the passing neighborhoods from the F train window. He smiled as the train passed over a playground below, "Yo! I'm going to kill these cats on the court when I get back!"

I sat with my arms folded, my tie resting on top of my forearms, slightly frustrated that I would have to skip my lunch break. "What position do you play?"

Dominic turned away from the window and slouched in the hard plastic seat, "Mostly power forward, I guess. . . . I don't know. You know nobody plays any positions on the court." Rubbing his hands over his overgrown afro, "But I got mad handle, though!"

"Yeah, everybody got handle," I said sarcastically.

"No for real, I'm like my boy Starbury."

I focused my gaze on the passing neighborhoods, "You know we have to stop at your school before we go to your house, right?"

Dominic's grin disappeared. "Come on, Mister. Can't I go home first?"

"It's Trevor. And no, you can't go home first. Judge's orders. I have to re-enroll you."

"Come on, man. I smell like shit!" Tugging on the front of his hooded sweatshirt, he said, "These clothes is mad dirty. I haven't showered in days . . ."

Turning back towards the window to catch his reflection, he remarked, "And I need someone to shape up my shit, y'naw mean?"

I laughed to myself momentarily, "Seriously Dominic. Let's just get it done, and then you can rest, shower, shape up, whatever."

Horror entered his eyes as he began to whisper, "But there's going to be girls there."

Standing up to tuck in my shirt and adjust my tie, I continued, "It's the next stop, Dominic."

Dominic turned away from me and slapped a collection of rolled up 8"x11" sheets of paper against his other hand. As the train slowed to a stop, he stood and pulled his beltless jeans up high enough to walk. After grabbing a small garbage bag filled with clothes from the seat next to him, he walked past me without saying a word.

We walked silently to an area high school in the Midwood neighborhood of Brooklyn. After filling out some forms in the administrators' office inside the school, Dominic was eager to get out of plain sight, "Hey, Mr."

"It's Trevor."

"Mr. Trevor, I need to use the bathroom."

I glanced past some of the office secretaries, "Dominic, they're printing your schedule now. Let's just wait a second, and then you can go home."

Dominic's eyes widened, "Yo, I have to go now!"

Before I could answer, the high school principal walked into the hall and approached me directly while fiddling with something in his hands. "You're Dominic's social worker?"

"Court advocate, yes."

Glancing away from his hands and directly towards me, he continued, "Can we talk for a second?"

I looked over at Dominic who still had a desperate look on his face. I paused before I spoke, "Okay, go. But come right back to this spot; I still have to escort you home."

Without answering, Dominic ran down the hall while holding his pants up with one hand. The principal walked towards his office as I followed.

Short, husky and balding, the principal sat in his swiveling chair behind his desk. His desk faced the door in a command position. He motioned for me to sit in one of the hard chairs in front of his desk as he propped his feet up on the corner, "I needed to talk to you about Mr. Taylor."

"Okay, what about?"

The principal began to trim his fingernails with a scissor-shaped nail clipper. He leaned with intense focus inches away from his fingers, systematically pushing the shavings into a small pile on the desk in front of him, "Look, I know how these programs work. You take kids out of jail because you think you can fix them. Some of these kids are committing real crimes....Some of these kids are real thugs. In my opinion, you're not giving them enough time in jail to be scared of it. I think you guys baby these kids too much."

"Well, I wouldn't say that..."

"Let me finish." His intense gaze turned away from his fingernails and towards me. "Dominic is a nuisance. A trouble-maker. You guys can try all you want to fix him, but I don't think he's going to be anything but a thug." Pointing his nail clippers at me, "And let me tell you, if he messes up once—one small fight, one time mouthing off to a teacher—he's gone."

I turned my palms to the ceiling and lifted them off my lap, "Okay, sir. You've got to do what you've got to do. I'll escort him home today, and then we'll see what happens after that."

The principal turned his attention back towards his nails, "Yeah, we'll see."

I saw myself out of his office and waited in the spot where I told Dominic to return. Thirty minutes or so passed before I pieced together that Dominic hadn't gone to the bathroom at all and instead slipped out one of the back doors of the buildings.

I took the F train to its final stop and walked to Coney Island Houses to investigate his mother's apartment. She was expecting him, but hadn't seen him all day. Dominic had decided to run. Run from his court obligations and run from his sole care provider. Two weeks later he was arrested in downtown Brooklyn and ended up serving his original sentence of three years' imprisonment for armed robbery.

Had Dominic gone home that day, gone to school the next, and generally followed the mandates of the alternative-to-incarceration program, he could have avoided jail time altogether. For weeks I shook my head over how senseless it was that he couldn't just follow a few simple rules. I had seen him cry over his remand. He was quietly scared of imprisonment, but he couldn't take the few simple steps to avoid it. "Why couldn't he just follow the rules?" I wondered to myself.

Although they didn't make sense to an adult in his mid-twenties, Dominic's lapses in judgment were typical for an adolescent boy growing up in Brooklyn. Many have written about the abundance of poor choices we make during our teenage years, as compared to our childhood or adulthood years. Most refer to this collection of deviant behaviors as *juvenile delinquency*, a subfield of criminology treated separately because of the unique circumstances for said behavior and the laws customized to punish or prevent them.

Beginning in the 1930s, social scientists recognized that adolescent criminal behavior was worthy of separate study. "Wayward" youth and delinquent children separated from their families had been a concern for decades, but it wasn't until the Great Depression that juvenile crime began to spike. Society as a whole was taken aback by juvenile delinquency because "children" had always been viewed as too innocent to engage in criminal behavior. But crime rates during the 1930s made the study of the uniqueness of juvenile delinquency unavoidable.

In an essay by Clifford Shaw and Henry McKay in 1932, they wondered if "broken homes" contributed to juvenile delinquency. At the time, they defined a broken home as a "death of one or both parents, divorce, desertion, or separation of parents."[1] This theory stipulated that the breakdown of family structure would cause youth to lash out against society. It insinuated that adolescents were not capable of wrong doing on their own, but needed some sort of a "push."

Decades later in David Matza's *Delinquency and Drift* (1964), he would agree that the 1930s represented an acceleration in juvenile crime due to a "gentle weakening of moral ties" in American society.[2] According to Matza, because of inconsistent legal codes and the cultural messages addressing right and wrong behavior, adolescents tended to "drift" back and forth between moral obligation and delinquency. The family unit was the key component to understanding the causal forces behind youthful waywardness in the early studies of delinquency.

Many scholars agreed that it was the family that taught children the most basic rules of society, and therefore was crucial in preventing delinquent behavior. In Travis Hirschi's *Causes of Delinquency* (1969), he regarded parenting and attachment to family as the greatest preventative force. According to Hirschi, "Control theory assumes that the bond of affection for conventional persons is a major deterrent to crime. The stronger this bond, the more likely the person is to take it into account when and if he contemplates a criminal act."[3] In other words, if a child is not able to create an emotional investment in his/her parents, then that child would be hard-pressed to invest in society. There is no emotional connection to a stranger, therefore, it becomes easier to *victimize* a stranger.

Most policy-oriented sociologists would agree that the family is the most difficult institution to investigate and legislate for, yet it is the most influential in the shaping of young minds. Government can put "parental advisory" labels on video games and music, or put truancy laws into place to keep kids in school, but it has no control over *how* a parent raises his/her children.

This begs to wonder if a lack of family, or deviant exposure through family, has a greater negative influence on juvenile delinquency. According to Hirschi,

> A persistent image in delinquency theory is that of a child *already* without a family—at least without a family whose unhappiness is of concern to him. . . . Since most delinquent acts are committed outside of the home, since a few delinquencies are committed at parental urging, and since most detected acts cause parents embarrassment and/or inconvenience, it is not surprising that an image of the delinquent as not only physically but emotionally free of his parents has developed.[4]

Scholars often assume that adolescents are delinquent because they do not follow the rules of their families; but it may be more of a matter of flaws in family structure. In Shaw and McKay's study of hundreds of youth from broken homes, they concluded that "the foregoing data suggest that we must look for these influences in the more subtle aspects of family relationships rather than in the formal break in the family organization."[5]

Family-oriented theories tend to neglect that youth may be learning deviant behaviors in the confines of their own homes and/or from their families. In Edwin Sutherland and Donald Cressey's "Theory of Differential Association," they claim that "criminal behavior is learned."[6] Most scholars would use Differential Association to describe neighborhood influence, but a person's home can also be a place to acquire "an excess of definitions" favorable to the violation of law. Whether through family, neighbors, or friends, adolescents are likely to learn about socially acceptable behavior through intimate groups.

Another impact on teenage deviant behavior is that of peer influence. The transition from childhood to adolescence often involves the transferring of norms learned in a family context to the norms learned amongst one's peers. Adult offenders tend to act on their own free will, while delinquent teens are often pressured by their friends. Of course, autonomous identity formation is particular to adolescence as teenagers are engaged in the process of separating oneself from one's childhood and attempting to forge a path towards adult independence.

Autonomy is often sought through risk-taking behavior and attachment to the group identity of one's peers. Whereas pre-pubescent children often adopt the cultural identity of their families, teens seek the approval and validation that comes from popular classmates and neighborhood idols. According to Peggy C. Giordano (et al) in their study of "Friendships and Delinquency," "psychological studies often equate 'peer relations' with sociometric rank (i.e. popularity), usually within the classroom setting."[7] Teenage preoccupation with moving up in sociometric rank often outweighs other priorities, and therefore, lends itself to deviant behavior as teens earn their way into the in-crowd.

Adolescent friendships tend to be grounded in emotion (rather than rationality). Teens follow peer-leaders strictly out of loyalty rather than what is right for them personally. Personal responsibility and doing the "right thing" often robs teens of status opportunities and chances to move up in rank. Therefore, friendships are often earned and validated by "loyalty in the face of trouble."[8] Teens may engage in crime together, get arrested together, and lie for each other just to preserve the friendship. This type of loyalty is unseen in adults, and often defines the key ingredients to peer pressure.

Mark Konty and Charles Peek (2003) would claim that "reams of research data demonstrate that most delinquents have delinquent friends."[9] In their study of delinquent teens, Konty and Peek believe that teens commit delinquent acts because "association with deviant peers provides a status opportunity, and status is a highly important goal for most adolescents." Crime is sometimes the result of just trying to *get in* to popular peer groups, and other times to maintain one's social status after they have been accepted by the group. This would explain why street gangs are mostly comprised of youth, and some adolescent deviant behaviors do not "make sense" to adults (who have stronger self-confidence that does not rely on the opinions of others).

As a result of seeking social status among popular peers, teens are more likely to engage in criminal behavior. According to Greg Weaver, "No longer a child but not yet an adult, the adolescent seeks to achieve autonomy by engaging in behavior that may be viewed as inappropriate."[10] The most common behaviors associated with autonomous detachment from childhood are drug use, underage alcohol consumption, and underage sexual activity. Of course, drug and alcohol use increases the likelihood of deviant and/or criminal activity.

According to the *Juvenile Offenders and Victims* 2006 Report, teens tend to engage in more daily drug use and experiment with unknown drugs compared to their adult counterparts.[11] And this in turn "increases the likelihood of engaging in unprotected sex or other acts that increase the risk of sexually transmitted diseases or trading sexual favors for drugs."[12] Of course, much of what we would label as "deviant" for adolescents tends to incorporate legal activities for adults (minus illicit drug consumption). Asserting that you are no longer a child can be proven through adult behaviors; and racing into the sexiest of adult behaviors makes a strong case for autonomy.

Strangely enough, adolescent deviant behavior—although generally universal—is more acute amongst boys. Many have wondered if this is a by-product of biology and/or of masculine socialization. According to Daniel Mears (et al) in their study of the "gender gap in delinquency," they claim that "gender is one of the strongest and most frequently documented correlates of delinquent behavior."[13] Boys represent close to 90 percent of all juvenile detainees and the majority of arrests. "Males commit more offenses than females at every age, within all racial or ethnic groups examined to date, and for all but a handful of offense types that are peculiarly female."[14]

Amongst all factors contributing juvenile delinquency, "being a boy" appears to be the most significant. But most scholars would not chalk this up to the effects of testosterone or possessing a y chromosome, for example. Mears (et al) claim that "males and females differ in their rates of delinquency because they are *differentially exposed* to the *same* criminogenic conditions."[15] Like Sutherland (in his Differential Association theory), they put a tremendous amount of weight on the frequency of exposure to delinquent peer groups. According to this thinking, boys are more likely to have delinquent friends, are more likely to "stay outside" later, and are more likely to have increased pressure on them to be delinquent to maintain status.

Many of these factors are influenced by families—which are more lenient when it comes to nightly curfew—and neighborhood influence—which tends to tolerate "hanging out" on the street more so than girls. In regards to the *pro-social* behavior of girls, Mears (et al) would claim that "females ordinarily possess something that acts as a barrier to inhibit or block the influence of delinquent peers."[16]

Scholars of gender studies would agree that biology influences the behavior of boys and girls less so than gender socialization. Particularly when it comes to autonomous expression, deviance and aggressive criminal behaviors are more associated with masculinity; whereas, "being good" are the more pro-social behaviors associated with girls and femininity. But oddly enough, the criminal expressions of masculinity tend to wear off when young boys reach maturity.

With more frequency in recent scholarship, delinquency has been deemed a "teenage thing." Crimes that seem illogical tend to wane in frequency as both boys and girls approach adulthood. As a result, more scholars are exploring the biological influences that affect adolescents exclusively. Biological determinism is dangerous territory, to say the least. Social scientists loathe the idea of repeating the claims of Cesare Lombroso and the "Italian School," as Social Darwinism has been taboo subject matter for decades.

More recently, sociologists have been warming up to the idea of considering biological impulses and their influence on juvenile delinquency. Rather than the continued exploration of genetics, race, or sex, some have been examining the effects of brain function on adolescent deviant behavior. Many neuroscientists conclude that the pre-frontal cortex—the part of the brain that controls most of our pro-social decision-making—is the last part of the brain to develop, and does not fully mature until we are close to twenty-five years old. Jay Geidd of the National Institute of Health claims that "it's sort of unfair to expect [adolescents] to have adult levels of organizational skills or decision making before their brain is finished being built."[17] Teens have the same cognitive capacity as adults, but in social situations teens tend to make more emotional decisions rather than thinking things through.

Also important in the discussion of biological impulse are the hormonal cocktails new to pubescent teens. Testosterone—which tends to increase tenfold in the first couple of years in puberty for boys—is responsible not only for increased muscle and bone mass, but increased energy and aggressivity. Estrogen—responsible for the growth of sex organs in girls—can also have an impact on decision-making as young girls attempt to solicit courtship from young boys. Like most species in nature, young boys use new found energy and libido to put on masculine displays as females gaze on. These displays could be as innocent as winning a sporting event, or as deviant as winning a fist fight.

Teenagers have the tough task of dealing with strong new impulses, while possessing very poor impulse control (in the form of an underdeveloped prefrontal cortex). Combined with added social pressure and the battle for sociometric status climbing, it is no surprise that adolescents make "dumb" decisions that lead to law-breaking behavior. That being said, adolescent deviant behavior should actually be *expected* from those in the throes of puberty. This is a time of exploring new found impulses and experimenting with the secrets of adulthood. But there are some teens who are more excessive in their expression of deviance.

For most people, deviant behavior dissipates as they begin to reach full maturity. For a select few, delinquency continues into one's adult years and is usually present before puberty. In Terrie E. Moffit's (et al) study of "antisocial behavior in males," they identify two types of juvenile delinquents: "adolescent-limited" youth (AL) and "life-course persistent" youth (LCP).[18] AL youth are quite the norm amongst adolescent boys. Deviance and/or delinquent behavior begin with the onset of puberty and then tend to fade as one enters his/her adult years. Moffit (et al) portrays juvenile delinquency as a natural reaction to the combination of new impulses and poor impulse control featured in pubescent development. AL teens typically engage in status offenses—such as underage drinking or smoking—but at times engage in illegal activity such as "vandalism, shoplifting, buying or selling stolen goods, carrying a weapon, using marijuana, (or) drunk driving."[19]

More rare, yet more concerning, are LCP youth who tend to exhibit signs of serious emotional disturbance (SED) before puberty and continue delinquent behavior into their adult years. "Boys on the LCP path have more violence. . . . [and] psychopathic traits." Like other neuro-scientific studies, Moffit (et al) recognize impairments in brain development as the cause for some of the most exceptional delinquent acts. "LCP antisocial behavior begins early in childhood because subtle neuro-psychological dysfunctions disrupt normal development of language, memory, and self-control, producing a toddler with cognitive delay and a difficult, under-controlled temperament."[20] These delays can lead to frustration in toddlers and can eventually manifest into years of conduct disorder, bullying, and other forms of violent behavior. The "over the top" juvenile delinquent—those that find themselves operating outside of peer influence—often have untraceable influences in their social environment, and now we can see that much of this behavior is the result of biological influences.

Much of the literature on juvenile delinquency acknowledges adolescent deviant behavior as an inevitable norm. Pubescent impulse, peer pressure, and the quest for autonomous identity construction make for a potent recipe for hazardous behaviors. Especially for young males—whose bodies push them towards greater aggressivity; and status opportunities drive them to prove one's manhood—influences often lead to criminal behavior compared to the non-criminal deviant behavior of young girls. As is said by Konty and Peek, "The male identity of toughness provokes risky male behavior in some circumstances because such behavior promotes this element of the male identity. The more risky the consequences, the better it supports a tough male identity."[21]

Family relations, neighborhood influence, and school structure matter even still, which is why the criminal justice system and human services agencies can play a role in curbing adolescent criminal behavior. There will always be the exceptional few who exhibit sociopathic traits from a young age, and their path to a healthy lifestyle involves more psychiatric remedies. But for the vast majority of youth (both male and female) delinquency can be impeded—not through the continued trend of increased incarceration—but rather through programs that divert youth away from detention and towards initiatives that help them to cope with the myriad of influences that lead to delinquency in the first place.

Diversion Programs as a Rehabilitative Tool

The term *diversion* is used in the legal system to describe when an alleged offender is provided with the opportunity to obviate detention, incarceration, and sometimes even a guilty conviction. Albert Roberts (2004) defines diversion programs "as any process that is used by components of the criminal justice system (police, prosecution, courts, corrections) whereby [alleged offenders] avoid formal . . . court processing and adjudication."[22] Eligibility for diversion is determined on a case-by-case basis after an individual is deemed worthy of a chance to "prove" him/herself, or if an individual is determined not to be a "flight risk" or a "danger to the community." At times, the legal system allows certain individuals to walk away from formal court processing without having to experience the negative labeling of a felony conviction or the damaging effects of incarceration.

In many instances, diversion programs are preferable for adolescent criminal offenders as they are seen as less likely to recidivate after receiving services. Diversion is also seen as a logical option because youth are impressionable. As said by Roberts,

> The major objective of many of the early diversion programs was to provide a structured, community-based alternative to incarceration so that petty offenders and status offenders would not be exposed to the corrupting influences of the more hardened multiple offenders who populate juvenile institutions.[23]

Many court judges use diversion programs to avoid the manufacturing habitual recidivists and with the hope of creating good citizens.

Diversion programs are nothing new. The use of probation (which comes from the Latin word *probare,* which by definition means a "period of proving") for adult offenders has been around for more than a century and a half. More than 4.1 million people are under probation supervision in the United States, which is nearly three times the amount of felons serving sentences in prison.[24]

Joan Petersilia (1998) accurately defined probation as "a court-ordered disposition alternative through which an adjudicated offender is placed under the control, supervision and care of a probation staff member in lieu of imprisonment, so long as the probationer meets certain standards of contact."[25] Although probation is a post-adjudicated sanction, it said to be a practical alternative to imprisonment as it is one-tenth of the cost of incarceration, it allows offenders to remain active (and employed) in their own communities, and the negative socialization that occurs in prisons can be avoided.

The very first instance of probation took place in Boston, Massachusetts in 1841 by a humble shoe-maker named John Augustus. Augustus would post bail mostly for drunkards and vagrants, and then attempt to rehabilitate them in his own home by instilling a Protestant work ethic. Only a handful of offenders were said to abscond, which set the standard for a very high success rate. According to Petersilia, Augustus created the model that we still use today. "Virtually every basic practice of probation was originally conceived by him. . . . He developed the ideas of the presentence investigation, supervision conditions, social casework, reports to the court, and revocation of probation."[26]

As the popularity of probation began to gain momentum entering the twentieth century, court judges determined it to be most useful for juvenile delinquents. "By 1927, almost all the states had enacted juvenile court laws, and a juvenile probation system had been developed in every state except Wyoming."[27] For adults and adolescents, court judges had to determine the types of crimes worthy of a second chance (or period of proving). Historically, probation supervision has been used as a punishment for petty crimes or class C or D felonies. As the 1900s progressed, juveniles were deemed worthy of supervision as a sanction for most of their criminal acts.

Since the 1930s, diversion for juvenile delinquents at times were used pre-adjudication, which allowed adolescents to walk away without a criminal record. The Crime Prevention Bureau of New York City in the 1930s received police referrals for "wayward minors." Without the stigma of a criminal conviction, these minors usually received some sort of social work intervention.

By the 1960s, elements of the juvenile justice system were concerned about the criminal socialization of youth, and as a result President of the United States Lyndon B. Johnson created the Commission on Law Enforcement and Administration of Justice in part to investigate the best practices for punishing and rehabilitating juvenile delinquents. A 1965 report suggested that "in place of the formal system, dispositional alternatives to adjudication must be developed for dealing with juveniles, including agencies to provide and coordinate services and procedures to achieve necessary control without unnecessary stigma."[28] This report also suggested increased use of juvenile diversion programs.

According to Albert Roberts, "The main objectives of juvenile diversion were to (a) avoid labeling, (b) reduce unnecessary detention and incarceration, (c) reduce repeat offenses, (d) provide counseling and other services, and (e) lower justice system costs."[29] Status offense cases and juvenile adjudication were supposed to be cut in half by the mid-1980s, but by then the criminal justice system was moving through a wholesale change which focused more on punishment.

Oddly enough by the 1990s, juvenile arrests and incarceration were increasing three-fold compared to the 1960s. Yet, there was room for diversions, even if it came with a conviction. According to Patricia Torbet (1996), by 1993, 56 percent of all adjudicated cases received probation.[30] But also by the mid-1990s, the debate over the effectiveness of probation was in full swing.

Many departments dedicated to probation supervision are said to be overloaded and lacking the tools necessary to do their jobs sufficiently. In New York City, juvenile probation officers are said to have caseloads of 54 clients each. Adult probation officers have an average of 113. Many appreciate the principles of probation, but are not sold on the practice. Even tough-on-crime/pro-incarceration writer John DiIulio, Jr. wrote in 1997 that the criminal justice system should "not abolish probation and parole, but . . . reinvent them."[31]

As many are concerned about the effectiveness of probation (and community supervision), most writers on the subject do see the potential. Torbet suggests that "the mission of probation will need to evolve even further to respond not only to juvenile offenders but also to the community."[32] As a result of the desire for community supervision—without a real administrative capacity for it—ATI programs certainly have a place within the juvenile justice system. As community supervision grows in popularity—whether through electronic monitoring or neighborhood based rehabilitation efforts—non-profit ATIs offer programs with even smaller recidivism rates for even less the cost. As we progress through the beginning of the twenty-first century, juvenile part judges are giving more consideration to community-based non-profit programs.

Notes

1. Shaw, Clifford R. and Henry D. McKay. (May 1932) "Are Broken Homes a Causative Factor in Juvenile Delinquency?" *Social Forces.* Vol. 10, No. 4. Pp. 514-524.

2. Matza, David. *Delinquency and Drift.* New Brunswick, N.J.: Transaction Publishers, 1990, (1964).

3. Hirschi, Travis. "Attachment to Parents." From *Readings in Juvenile Delinquency and Juvenile Justice.* (Edited by Thomas Calhoun & Constance Chapple). Upper Saddle River, N.J.: Prentice Hall, 2003.

4. Hirschi, p. 134.

5. Shaw and McKay, p. 524.

6. Sutherland, Edwin and Donald R. Cressey. "A Theory of Differential Association." *Criminology,* 8th ed. J.B. Lippincott Company, 1970. Pp. 75-77.

7. Giordano, Peggy C., Stephen A. Cerkovich, and M.D. Pugh. "Friendships and Delinquency." From *Readings in Juvenile Delinquency and Juvenile Justice.* (Edited by Thomas Calhoun & Constance Chapple). Upper Saddle River, N.J.: Prentice Hall, 2003.

8. Peggy Giordiano, et al, p. 283.

9. Konty, Mark A., and Charles W. Peek. "Label-Seeking for Status: Peers, Identities, and Domains of Deviance." From *Readings in Juvenile Delinquency and Juvenile Justice.* (Edited by Thomas Calhoun & Constance Chapple). Upper Saddle River, N.J.: Prentice Hall, 2003.

10. Weaver, Greg S. "Juvenile Delinquency and Drug Use." From *Readings in Juvenile Delinquency and Juvenile Justice.* (Edited by Thomas Calhoun & Constance Chapple). Upper Saddle River, N.J.: Prentice Hall, 2003.

11. Snyder, Howard and Melissa Sickmund. *Juvenile Offenders and Victims: 2006 National Report.* Washington, D.C.: Office of Juvenile Justice and Delinquency Prevention, 2006.

12. Weaver, p. 247.

13. Mears, Daniel P., Matthew Ploeger, and Mark Warr. "Explaining the Gender Gap in Delinquency: Peer Influence and Moral Evaluations of Behavior." From *Readings in Juvenile Delinquency and Juvenile Justice.* (Edited by Thomas Calhoun & Constance Chapple). Upper Saddle River, N.J.: Prentice Hall, 2003.

14. Mears, et al, p. 356.

15. Mears, et al, p. 357.

16. Mears, et al, p. 358.

17. Juvenile Justice Center Report. "Adolescence, Brain Development, and Legal Culpability." (January 2004). Attained from American Bar Association website: http://www.abanet.org/crimjust/juvjus/Adolescence.pdf.

18. Moffitt, Terrie E., Avshalom Caspi, Nigel Dickson, Phil Silva, and Warren Stanton (March 1996). "Childhood-onset Versus Adolescent-onset Antisocial Conduct Problems in Males: Natural History from Ages 3 to 18 Years." *Development and Psychopathology.* (8), pp. 399-424.

19. Moffitt, et al, p. 410.
20. Moffitt, et al, p. 402.
21. Konty, Mark A. and Charles W. Peek, p. 326.
22. Roberts, Albert R. "The Emergence and Proliferation of Juvenile Diversion Programs." *Juvenile Justice Sourcebook: Past, Present and Future.* [Albert R. Roberts, Ed]. New York: Oxford University Press, 2004.
23. Roberts, Albert [1], p. 184.
24. Clear, Todd R., George F. Cole, and Michael D. Reisig. *American Corrections.* Eighth Ed. Belmont, Calif.: Thomson Wadsworth, 2009.
25. Petersilia, Joan (1998). "Probation in the United States." *Perspectives, Spring 1998.* Pp. 42-49.
26. Petersilia, Joan, p. 33.
27. Roberts, Albert R. "The Emergence of the Juvenile Court and Probation Services." *Juvenile Justice Sourcebook: Past, Present and Future.* [Albert R. Roberts, Ed]. New York: Oxford University Press, 2004.
28. Roberts [1], Albert, p. 186.
29. Roberts [1], Albert, p. 190.
30. Torbet, Patricia McFall. "Juvenile Probation: The Workhorse of the Juvenile Justice System." Report prepared by the U.S. Department of Justice, Office of Juvenile Justice and Delinquency Prevention, March 1996. Retrieved on October 4, 2010 from OJJDP website: http://www.ncjrs.gov/pdffiles/workhors.pdf.
31. DiIulio, John J., Jr. "Reinventing Parole and Probation." *The Brookings Review,* Vol. 15, No. 2 (Spring 1997), pp. 40-42.
32. Torbet, Patricia McFall, p. 4.

Chapter 3: ATIs and the Deferred Sentence

Outside of part 16 in Brooklyn Supreme Court, I stood with Reggie's mother coaching her towards her next step. "Look, we've done all that we can do. Now we just have to walk in there and hope that he gets a light sentence."

She clutched her purse a little tighter before pleading, "But you don't understand. My baby didn't do it. He couldn't hurt a fly. He's not guilty."

Placing my hand on her shoulder, I continued, "Ms. Johnson, like I said, we've done everything we can. He didn't show up to the program, and therefore, he violated the terms of his agreement."

Pining further, tears began to well up in her eyes. "But my boy didn't do it! He's not capable of something like that. There must be something we can do."

Like many mothers of court-involved youth, Ms. Johnson did not fully comprehend the legal process. Even though she was present when her son agreed to the terms of his conditional release and postponed sentence, she still did not understand that a plea bargain meant the terms of agreement could not be rescinded. I exhaled a brief sigh before I continued, "Ms. Johnson, he pleaded guilty months ago. And to the court, that means he did it. There's no way out of this now. We just have to hope . . ."

"But he didn't do it! I know Reggie . . . He couldn't have."

Before I could continue, a court officer opened the door and stuck his head out, "Johnson!" I motioned with my eyes that we needed to step inside. Ms. Johnson followed me inside the court room and then sat down in the pews behind the defense attorney's table. Dressed in a light-brown prison jumpsuit, Reggie stood with his head crooked to one side, his hands shackled behind his back. He was flanked by a court officer on one side and his defense attorney on the other.

The judge sat silently at his bench, thumbing through a manila folder full of paper. Slowly grazing his hand from his brow to the back of his head, he let out a big sigh. He stopped on one page, held it up to the ceiling light, adjusted his glasses, and whispered to himself, "Geez." After a couple more pages, he closed the folder and removed his eye glasses, "Okay, let's get this going." The judge glanced at the court officer and nodded, signaling him to remove Reggie's handcuffs. The court clerk stood up. "New York versus Reginald Johnson. You may be seated."

The judge brushed his brow once more before addressing the defendant, "Mr. Johnson. On March 2nd you plead guilty to robbery in the first degree." Putting his glasses back on, he removed a sheet of paper from the file, "The police investigation showed that you held up a Chinese food delivery person with a 747 Hunter's Point Folder Knife. You were able to seize his all of his property, including $74 in cash and the food he was delivering." The judge then looked up from the paper and over his glasses, "You then went on to assault the man with your fists, and then you fled the scene. You still admit to this?"

Reggie, who had been sitting silently—eyebrows scowling—let out a short reply, "Yes."

The judge stared an extra moment before continuing, "Mr. Johnson, I gave you a chance to redeem yourself in one of the best ATI programs in the city, and you failed to do that. You understand that if you completed the program, you could have earned Y.O. status and five years probation?"

Reggie was as still as a statue. "Yes."

"Mr. Milton, are there any additional comments that you would like to add to your organization's court report?"

I stood, "Only that he has not been present for three weeks, he hasn't been on time for curfew for more than a week, and . . ." I paused, trying to find something positive to say.

"Mr. Milton."

". . . And he had a positive tox screening on April 28th, Your Honor."

The judge looked to the table on the left side of the room, "Assistant D.A., do you have anything to add before I sentence him?"

The assistant district attorney stood, briefly flipping to a single page in her own file and then spoke, "Yes, Your Honor, the district attorney recommends the maximum of ten years, as he is a violent felon and someone who has shown no remorse throughout this entire process." She closed the file before sitting down. "Nothing further, Your Honor."

The judge looked to the defense's table, "Counsel?"

The defense attorney, a tall, slim African American man, stood and adjusted his suit, "If I might have a *few* words, Your Honor."

"You may."

Looking down towards Reggie, the attorney began, "Your Honor, the district attorney's office looks at Mr. Johnson here and sees a violent animal; a hunter of sorts only looking to find his next victim." He then put his hand on Reggie's shoulder and quieted his voice. "When I look at Reggie, I see a sixteen-year-old boy; a teenage boy who's trying to make it in his neighborhood. A boy who is scared of what his friends might think of him if he doesn't act 'hard.' A boy who never had a father figure in his life to guide him to the right path. A boy . . ."

The judge interrupted, "Counsel, what are your recommendations?"

"Your Honor, all I mean to say is, if we put this boy away, this will ruin his life. We will be making him into a career criminal. And that will be bad for him, *and* bad for all of us. He's just a little boy. A boy that will become a man in prison. A boy . . ."

"Counsel."

"Your Honor, the public defender's office is recommending the minimum sentence of one year, sir."

The judge removed his glasses, "Mr. Johnson, please stand up." The court officer grabbed Reggie by the back of the arm and pulled him to his feet. The defense attorney and I stood in anticipation of the sentence. Reggie stood frighteningly still as the judge began to explain his decision, "You know, Mr. Johnson, I deal with kids like you everyday. They come from rough neighborhoods; broken homes." Pointing with his glasses, "They stand in front of me with that same hard look, thinking they can intimidate me." The judge leaned back in his chair, "But I know deep down you're just a kid. Someone who can still use some guidance. That's why I send you to programs like this one, because we all deserve a second chance. But I have to maintain a line. I've been burned before when I've been too lenient on kids. Almost ruined my career. I've got to hold *you* to your word, and I have to make sure that I am a man of *my own* word. Now, I made a deal with the D.A., and you had a second chance. A second chance to . . ."

Without warning, Reggie interrupted, "Why the fuck are we wasting all this time? I don't need to hear how you feel about me. I don't give a fuck. Why don't you just shut the fuck up and sentence me!"

For a short moment the court room stood still, as if frozen in time. Not a single sound was made. The judge's eyes were pried wide open with amazement. The defense attorney and I simultaneously looked to the ground and slapped our foreheads. Ms. Johnson burst into tears behind me. The judge slowly turned his head towards the court stenographer, "Did you get that?" The stenographer nodded, eyes equally as wide.

Reggie spoke one more time, "For real. What the fuck are we waiting for?"

Several strangers in the back of the court room began to gasp as the judge slapped his hand on the bench; his eyes back to their normal squint, "All right, Mr. Johnson, as you wish." He motioned for the court officer to cuff him one more time. The judge closed his file, "Reginald Johnson, I am going to sentence you to the maximum allowed for your crime. Ten years with the possibility of parole after eight and a half. Thank you." As the judge knocked his gavel, Ms. Johnson screamed, "No! He didn't do it!"

As the court officer began to move him away from the defense table, Reggie turned to me looking for some sort of encouragement. I had very little to offer. "Hang in there . . . Reggie." As the officer escorted Reggie towards the holding room in the back, I could see tears rolling down his face. He raised his shoulder to wipe his left eye. Before passing through the door frame, he looked back towards his mother and then pointed his head back towards the floor.

In my line of work as a court advocate, Reggie was exceptionally arrogant. Most of the participants were afraid to go to prison, and as a result were afraid to upset the presiding judge. Unlike many of the clients, Reggie was brash, and frankly foolish, in a situation that could have changed the course of his life. But like many of the clients, he was a first time offender, and therefore someone deemed worthy of a second chance. Whether the individual teen chooses to comply with the program—and in Reggie's case if they choose to insult the intelligence of the judges—is a gamble.

There is a complicated set of reasoning that goes into the decision to allow an adolescent offender a chance at rehabilitation in their own communities. As is said in the Juvenile Offender Handbook, "There are certain cases that appear to warrant a sanction more onerous than probation, but for which a sentence of incarceration seems unduly harsh. In such cases, the juvenile offender may be required to participate in an alternative to incarceration (ATI) program or community-based program as a precondition to receiving a sentence of probation or—most often—as an express condition to a sentence of probation."[1]

The Judges in Supreme Court, Criminal Court, and Family Court are the gatekeepers. In a regular adult case, if a person has been charged with a serious crime, it is they who determine if a person is "flight risk" or a "danger to the community." For adolescent offenders they have to take the same criteria into account, while simultaneously measuring what is best for the teen. The presence of an ATI program in the court system is contingent upon the invitation of enthusiastic Supreme, Criminal or Family Court judges. This is one of the major reasons why there is not a significant ATI presence in the boroughs of Queens and Staten Island. The judges in Queens who handle the juvenile cases prefer to use the Department of Probation for community supervision, while the judges in Staten Island typically prefer placement.

Both for the safety of the community and the existence of community-based programs, the relationship between ATI program representatives and the judges who decide the adolescent's fate must have clear channels of communication and an agreed upon strategy for the young offender's rehabilitation. Most judges who hear juvenile cases would not consider an ATI for an offender who has committed any "serious felonies," such as murder, manslaughter, arson, assault with a deadly weapon, or any sexual assault charges. Judges have a reputation to uphold and an obligation to public safety. They have to sort through each presentence investigation in order to determine if the youth would be a good candidate for community-based treatment.

When I began my research in 2004, I set out to interview the judges with whom I had worked with as a Court Advocate. Bronx Supreme Court Justice John Moore said in our initial interview, "I have an instinct for reading a file and determining if the kid is eligible for an ATI. If the kid is less actively involved in the crime—for example, if there is no gun possession, but rather a lookout in a robbery—then he is most likely to be considered." As a result, many of the youth in ATI programs have second and third degree felony or misdemeanor charges: the most common being robbery in the second degree and drug possession (in Supreme Court); and trespassing and "incorrigibility" (in Family Court). Judges look for teens "who were in the wrong place at the wrong time," or look to be "one-time offenders."

Like the justices of the past who were active participants in the Child Saving Movement, judges that are enthusiastic about ATIs today believe that adolescents are capable of developing a new identity and more pro-social behavior. In a criminal justice system where the administrative codes make no distinction between a thirteen and a thirty-year-old felony offender, many judges believe that thirteen-year-olds can be more easily rehabilitated because they are hardwired for continued growth and learning. But it can be tricky at times to predict the behaviors of the most unpredictable segment of our population. As is said by Aaron Kupchik, "Court decision makers are unable to avoid the adolescents' immaturity, or to hold adolescent offenders fully culpable for their actions as suggested by the criminal justice model."[2]

Manhattan Supreme Court Justice Michael Corriero was very enthusiastic about the rehabilitative power of ATI programs. He explained that he preferred to look at ATIs as "an extension of the court, an unofficial probation department." When I sat with him, he expressed his disappointment in the allowable choices for sentencing. He was obligated to stick with the guidelines of the Juvenile Offender Law, but he claimed "the law does not explain the time that I am allowed to sentence." Therefore, when a Juvenile Offender or Youthful Offender is found guilty of a designated felony crime, he was allowed to postpone the sentence for up to a year.

Take for example, a hypothetical case of a fifteen-year-old found guilty of robbery in the second degree. The judge can sentence him to anywhere from five years probation to seven years incarceration. The decision is based on public safety and whether the teen shows potential for rehabilitation. For judges like Justice Corriero, in order to lessen the risk of recidivism (and the media backlash for making a poor decision), they prefer that the youth "earn" the sentence of probation by completing the mandates of an ATI program.

As a court advocate, I witnessed several youth charged with robbery or weapons possession (for example) given a choice: serve two years in a state correctional facility, or be monitored in your own community by the Department of Probation for five years. The sentence of probation was "conditioned" upon completing the requirements of a hand-chosen ATI program. If the adolescent offender agreed, then they would plea guilty to the crime as charged, sign a court agreement, and then they would be released to the program for twelve months.

The "conditions for release" were very similar to a typical probationer or parolee. The conditions often included, a) regular school attendance, b) remaining drug free, c) returning to one's place of residence by a designated time each evening, d) not accumulating any new charges (including status offenses), and e) maintaining regular attendance at the ATI program after school hours. It was up to the ATI program to monitor the teen's compliance with these conditions, and just like probation, if any of these conditions were violated, the deal was off and they would be sentenced to incarceration.

Most youth whom I worked with were given a crash course in personal responsibility as they had to maintain a seven-hour-a-day school schedule with homework, drug tests, curfew checks, random home visits, and regular sessions with the programs. This may actually be more difficult for a teenager than an adult, as they are constantly pressured by their friends to explore deviant behavior. There were a few, whom after doing twelve months in the program and then having to look forward to five years of probation supervision, would turn and say to me, "I should have taken the two years in jail."

A path which includes six years of criminal justice monitoring and program education is an arduous one, but one that may prove to be more beneficial than an initial dive into a pattern of perpetual incarceration. For many ATI clients, the expectations are already low from the beginning. Many come from similar backgrounds, backgrounds that are often detrimental to a good quality of life. I asked Bronx Supreme Court Justice John Moore to describe the background of a typical youth indicted in Criminal Court and he composed the following answer:

> There tends to be criminal history in the family. No father figure, or no meaningful interaction with their father. Sometimes the mother has issues with drugs. Poverty is *always* the case. Many have learning disabilities, which have not been identified. There is a *huge* lack of parenting. . . . You know, a colleague of mine once told me, "We're not rehabilitating these kids, we're *habilitating* them." Teaching them the most basic skills! It's not all of them; some parents try. Many have done something stupid out of peer influence. But this is an exception to the rule.[3]

In his description, Justice Moore identified poverty and weak family structure as major causal forces for juvenile delinquency. Stable family structure has been recognized as a deterrent to crime since the beginnings of the Chicago School. Park viewed "the breaking down of local attachments and the weakening of the restraints and inhibitions of the primary group . . . (as) largely responsible for the increase of vice and crime in great cities."[4] But some sociologists would argue that the media-induced breakdown of family structure is affecting urban and suburban, rich and poor. Yet some are able to come out of this *mainstream cultural deprivation* with better life chances.

When it comes to reform, advocates of rehabilitation are charged with reversing the effects of structural deprivation and the effects of poor family structure. Like Justice Moore, Judge Corriero recognized that these effects are *likely* to drive a young person to incarceration. "These kids tend to come from single-parent households. There's usually ACS [Administration for Children's Services] involvement. Typically, the parent is not working. The child is not doing well in school. . . . These are symptoms of an impoverished neighborhood. . . . There is also the legacy of slavery, unequal education, oppression and family breakdown. When you don't have an intact family, you have to struggle to flourish." Many judges in juvenile parts believe it is their mission to reverse the effects of structural deprivation and rehabilitate young people who are still learning.

For the judges who believe in the decriminalization of youthful behavior, ATIs provide an alternative to their administrative obligations. As Judge Moore said, they are useful because "they have a collective package together, services that are helpful to the individual." The successful rehabilitation of the individual is dependent upon the types of services they receive. Most ATI programs tend to provide skills that will connect them to the job market, the completion of their educational goals, and social skills for dealing with their environment. Not only are there many who are enthusiastic about ATIs, but many are also motivated by the perceived detriments that can be caused by habitual incarceration.

Fear of Prison Socialization

In the past couple of decades, there has been a growing literature on the effects of incarceration on community. Whereas, since the 1970s the criminal justice system has poured all of its resources towards punishment and deterrence, researchers are beginning to see the damage that incarceration has on a neighborhood safety rather than its perceived benefits. As Todd Clear wrote in his essay "Addition by Subtraction" (2002), "High levels of incarceration concentrated in impoverished communities have a destabilizing effect on community life, so that the most basic underpinnings of informal social control are damaged. This, in turn, reproduces the very dynamics that sustain crime."[5] By removing wage earners and other neighborhood figures, community ties begin to break down as this leaves families without income and residents without potential mentors.

But the original concept behind "addition by subtraction" is built around the claim that a neighborhood should see increased public safety if its worst elements are removed. Proponents of current policy would play up the 23 percent crime drop in the United States since the early 1990s in general—and the 46 percent crime drop in New York City in particular—as evidence of the effectiveness of the punishment/deterrence approach. Even if an individual family suffers from a wage-earning father's incarceration, that family's neighbors benefit greatly by worrying less about victimization. The individual family is just collateral damage for the greater good.

Between 1980 and 2000, as many inmates began to come back to communities after completing their sentences, a new problem emerged: prisoner reentry. Michael Jacobson defined prisoner reentry in *Downsizing Prisons* (2005) as "the hefty barriers encountered by ex-prisoners as they attempt to reintegrate themselves back into their communities."[6] Prisons may be frightening and undesirable places to be, but it seems that they are not preparing inmates to readjust to real community life. This creates a disruption not only to the ex-inmate—who finds it difficult to adjust to a changed world, or to find work in a job market that can legally discriminate against their criminal history—but it also disrupts the community as they are likely to deal with the ex-prisoner violating the law yet again.

Recidivism rates for men have remained steady at 80 percent for two decades, yet the criminal justice model has made few adjustments to fix this number. What is more concerning is that there seems to be a growing relationship between neighborhoods with high incarceration rates and prisons themselves. What kind of effect does it have on a neighborhood when a mass of individuals "trained" inside of prisons bring their prison skills back home? What are the things that are transferred from ex-inmates to their respective neighborhoods?

One motivation for the recent move back towards to medical model is the growing fear of the transference of *prison subculture.* The prison was designed to be a total institution with its own boundaries, rules, customs—and consequently its own folkways, norms—and eventually its own "culture." Since the 1940s, scholars have been studying and documenting the *inmate code.* In John Irwin and Donald Cressey's (1962) famous study of prison culture, they identified seven major "codes" of conduct between prisoners:

1) Do your own time
2) Be a stand up guy
3) Don't rat on other inmates
4) Don't exploit other inmates
5) Don't trust the guards
6) Settle conflict between inmates
7) Respect the "real" cons[7]

These are rules not designed and enforced by prison superintendents or corrections officers, but by the prisoners themselves. This is a code that allows for "doing your time" while remaining safe. Inmates were supposed to respect each others' boundaries, and this is a way to avoid prison violence.

The inmate code of the 1960s relied heavily on distrust of corrections officers and a respect for older inmates and "real cons" (convicts who have committed more serious offenses). As the prison population grew throughout the 1980s and 1990s, prisoners became more violent as a consequence of proving who is and who is not a "real con." As has been made popular in recent television shows and movies, prison has become an institution that hosts the most extreme and gruesome versions of interpersonal violence. As is said by Robert Johnson in his book *Hard Time* (2002), "The convict world is populated by men who doubt their worth as human beings and who feel they must constantly find occasions to 'prove' themselves. . . . The convict world is a world of continuing—and generally escalating—conflict. Aggrieved parties cannot afford to back down, for then they are seen as weak and hence vulnerable to more abuse. Violence is the convict's world as he establishes one's competence as a man who can survive in a human jungle."[8]

If "proving oneself" becomes a priority for individuals in prisons, then this invites large changes to the inmate code. If attacking a real con is a way to earn respect, then this gets added to the prison subculture (and subtracted from the old code). If sexual exploitation of a weaker inmate is a means of gaining power, then this can also become an addition. Gang violence, drug trade retaliation and sexual conquest are commonplace inside of prisons; joining one of these gangs an absolute necessity inside of maximum security facilities. Individual members of street gangs, such as the Crips and the Bloods, may find themselves united under the "Black Guerilla Family" for protection by race. White inmates—who may have never considered themselves racist before prison—are encouraged to join the "Aryan Brotherhood" for similar protection. If Sunday is the most segregated day of the week because of church attendance, then prisons are the most segregated institutions because of the perceived need for protection.

Irwin and Cressey's study is arguably outdated. Inmates' quest for respect has led to the degradation of some rules and the strengthening of others. In general, inmates continue to have a distrust of corrections officers and believe that "ratting someone out" (or "snitching," in today's vernacular) is a mortal sin. But respect for the rights of other inmates has waned and given way to personal desire for power. In T.J. Granack's essay "Welcome to the Steel Hotel: Survival Tips for Beginners" (2000), he offers the following as an updated version of the prison code:

1) Commit an honorable crime
2) Don't gamble
3) Never loan anyone anything
4) Make no eye contact
5) Pick your friends carefully
6) Fight and fight deprived
7) Mind your own business
8) Keep a good porn collection
9) Don't talk to staff, especially guards
10) Never snitch[9]

Granack suggests that by following these simple rules, a new inmate can decrease his chances of prison violence and continuous victimization. The odd key, of course, is that the inmate eventually has to accept that he will be challenged at some point.

Most corrections officials have stories about the techniques that prisoners use to seriously injure or murder each other. Whether it's making a knife out of a sharpened toothbrush, or a "baseball bat" out of a tightly wound newspaper, inmates put their free time and intelligence to use in order to survive. Outsiders believe that prisoners spend their time contemplating how to escape prison, when in reality they are contemplating how to escape prison violence.

Prison violence may be tolerated by corrections officials because of its perceived effect on deterrence. What rational thinking person would want to commit a crime if a prison sentence guarantees daily fights, stabbings, gang initiation, drug wars, and rape? Prison violence—as a branch of the criminal justice system—can be viewed as an effective tool for keeping crime rates low.

But there are those who are able to tolerate this violence; those that view surviving this "human jungle" as a badge of honor. Thus, this contributes to the growing fear that prisons are losing their penchant for deterrence and instead are manufacturing chronic offenders. This was the fear of the original Child Savers of the nineteenth century and the architects of the first prisons in the United States. Designers of the Walnut Street Jail (the first prison in the United States built in 1790) wanted to prevent prisoner fraternization altogether because of the fear that prisoners would trade criminal secrets. Now this has become a staple in prisons, and contemporary scholars are beginning to wonder if this is having an effect on communities.

In Jacob Stowell and John Byrne's article "Does What Happen in Prisons Stay in Prisons?" (2008), they challenge the notion of the *prison importation model.* This model suggests that prison violence exists because it is imported by violent criminals. Prisoner violence is a byproduct of violent communities. But the prison importation model does not take into account the violence that is produced by the circumstances of prison confinement. Whereas, if earning respect and proving oneself is unavoidable in prisons, then the prison is likely to produce violence regardless of prisoners' natural attitudes towards fighting. As is said by Stowell and Byrne, "Due to high levels of inmate release, it stands to reason that prison culture is likely to be 'exported' back into communities. More generally, [this research] suggest(s) that a reciprocal, or mutual reinforcing, association exists between prison and community cultures."[10]

If particular communities produce irregularly high rates of incarceration, then it stands to reason that prison violence becomes reciprocally connected to violence in the same communities. Inmate code—including "no snitch" expectations and willingness to act on violent impulse if tested—is exported into disadvantaged communities by ex-prisoners. "Activities [such] as gang involvement, drug dealing, and the situational use/threat of violence in prison may represent the primary 'skill set' of many of today's inmates. Once released from prison… faced with the same (or worsening) opportunity structure, it is not surprising that they continue to make what you and I might consider 'bad' choices."[11]

We can see the effects of *prison culture exportation* in popular culture today. From sagging jeans (caused by prison policy restricting use of belts because of high rates of suicide and violence against other inmates) to neck and face tattoos (originally clear indicators of prison gang affiliation), there exists evidence of prison subculture in segments of American culture that are not even crime-engaged. Urban, as well as wealthy suburban teens, are living by prison subculture: not backing down in fights and inventing hand gestures to "represent" their neighborhood.

Within our criminal justice system, there is a growing recognition that prisons may be manufacturing violent individuals, and in turn, creating more violence in poor communities. Stowell and Byrne concluded that "the institutions that were created to reduce violence and disorder in the community may actually be having the opposite effect on inmates both within institutions and in the 'communities' to which inmates return."[12] Our current prison structure may be creating an entire generation of *willing* frequent flyers to the prison system.

In the example at the beginning of the chapter, many saw the risk of putting Reggie Johnson away for ten years. Twenty-six year old Reggie is likely to be more violent, more hardened, and less likely to care for the concerns of his neighbors. But of course, the court system's hands are tied if an adolescent offender is a "danger to the community." Reggie was certainly on the cusp: a first time offender, but someone who cared too much for street respect. This is the court system's greatest difficulty when dealing with adolescents. As is said by Kupchik, "Court decision makers are unable to avoid the adolescents' immaturity, or to hold adolescent offenders fully culpable for their actions as suggested by the criminal justice model."[13]

Judges and ATI programs have to determine which adolescents are most likely to turn themselves around and avoid contact with prison subculture. As a court advocate, I also worked with a fifteen-year-old from Brownsville, Brooklyn. Brownsville has the second highest crime rate and the highest arrest rate in the city. Wendell—a Jamaican-born first-time offender from a single-parent home—was at a very pivotal moment in his life when I met him. He had been charged with second degree robbery after being present when a friend of his robbed an elderly woman. During my first intake interview with Wendell (inside of his home), I could see that he was caught between two worlds.

Wendell's mother was raising him on the strict working class values of Jamaican culture. He had a curfew, he had to do his homework, and he had to engage in small acts of respect while inside the home, like removing his hat upon entrance and calling me "sir" during my interview. In my eyes he was a polite boy who was sweet to his mother and did well in school. After our interview, he escorted me out of his apartment where I was able to see him interact with his friends. His attitude changed; his speech was more aggressive and included more curse words. He spoke about not caring "what my mom think about me." It's young boys like Wendell that Criminal Court judges and ATI programs search for: young boys who are involved in the criminal justice system, but have not crossed over to a permanent life of crime.

There are many in the ATI world that regard imprisonment as being detrimental to the growth of the teenage mind. Whereas, adult sentences are meant to scare non-crime engaged youth—and youth who are currently incarcerated—from ever committing crimes, it appears to be having the opposite effect. In an interview with Miles Jackson—then the Director of the Osborne Association—he reiterated his dislike of detaining youth, "OCFS and DJJ regard their role as baby-minding. Juveniles are just there to serve their time. These are institutions of confinement, using *coercion control* to control youth. But they don't promote self-control. ATIs, on the other hand, desire to promote the internalization of control mechanisms." It is this internalization that may help to build in youth the necessary tools to avoid prison subculture and a life of criminal behavior.

Judge Michael Corriero claimed that "being young is conducive to getting into trouble." His was a recognition that teenage life—and the boisterous posturing of teen boys in particular—is a temporary stage in life. He explained that "we can't criminalize adolescence. Social policy has to permit recovery from mistakes. Kids are going to be kids." This is why he is a big fan of ATI programs and is well aware the cycle that exposure to imprisonment can induce in young people.

Compared to past community support, community justice has been weakened by decades of New York's "tough on crime" policies. Justice Corriero—who served the juvenile part in Manhattan Supreme Court from 1992 to 2007—explained that when he was growing up, he had "mentors and teachers that cared. Parochial schools had an *interventionist attitude*. We moved to a culture that readily accepts single parents. The role of the government today should be to nurture the environment that children are raised in." He also understood the attraction to street crime, as he too "wanted to be like the guy in the 'Caddy' with all the girls" when he was walking the streets of Tribeca in the 1960s. Even the most successful members of our society recognize what is attractive about street life.

As adults, we assume that children understand that prison is a loathsome destination: "*I'm* afraid to go to prison, therefore, a child must be *doubly* afraid." We forget to teach teenagers this message. In an interview with Angel Rodriguez—Director of the Andrew Glover Program—he reiterated, "the corrections system tends to welcome them back. Punishment does not equal rehabilitation, therefore, they are not being taught that this system is bad for them. These kids go into jail and have 'burglary sessions.'" What should be of greatest concern to criminal justice officials today is the unintended creation of a young criminal class. Youth currently receive the message that there are social rewards for engagement in street life. And there are double rewards for surviving the "human jungle." We are at a point in history where young adults are returning home to their communities after long prison sentences, and they are being celebrated as "war heroes" by the young kids in the neighborhood. Youth also receive the message that the criminal justice system does not care about them, which may actually encourage *more* deviant behavior.

It is the duty of the court system and ATI programs to recognize the cultural forces at work—both mainstream and local—and to deliver a new message to youth still trying to establish their own identity. Thus far, we have followed the lead of writers, such as John Dilulio (1996), who claim that adolescent offenders are "morally poor." This would suggest that there is nothing that can be done to correct it. Teens hear this message and eventually succumb to the effects of labeling. But to redirect this new generation by understanding their desires and influences is key.

Notes

1.Warner, Eric. *The Juvenile Offender Handbook: A Comprehensive Guide to the "J.O. Law" and Related Statutes.* New York: Looseleaf Publications, 2007.

2. Kupchik, p. 15.

3. Interview with Justice John Moore, Bronx Supreme Court (Dec. 9, 2005).

4. Park, Robert. "The City: Suggestions for the Investigation of Human Behavior," *American Journal of Sociology, 20(5),* 1915.

5. Clear, Todd R. "The Problem with 'Addition by Subtraction': The Prison-Crime Relationship in Low-Income Communities." *Invisible Punishment: The Collateral Consequences of Mass Imprisonment.* Edited by Marc Mauer and Meda Chesney-Lind. New York, N.Y.: W.W. Norton & Company, 2002.

6. Jacobson, Michael. *Downsizing Prisons: How to Reduce Crime and End Mass Incarceration.* New York, N.Y.: New York University Press, 2005.

7. Irwin, John and Donald Cressey. "Thieves, Convicts, and the Inmate Culture." *Social Problems* 10 (1962): 145-157.

8. Johnson, Robert. *Hard Time: Understanding and Reforming the Prison.* Belmont, Calif.: Wadsworth, 2002.

9. Granack, T.J. "Welcome to the Steel Hotel: Survival Tips for Beginners." From *The Funhouse Mirror,* edited by Robert Gordon Ellis. Pullman, Wash.: Washington State University Press, 2000.

10. Stowell, Jacob I. & James M. Byrne. "Does What Happens in Prison Stay in Prison? Examining the Reciprocal Relationship between Community and Prison Culture." From *The Culture of Prison Violence.* Boston, Mass.: Pearson Education, 2008.

11. Stowell & Byrne, p. 36

12. Stowell et al, p. 28

13. Kupchik, p. 15

Chapter 4: Masculinity and the Magnetism of the Streets

When I moved from Boston to New York City in 2000, I settled in the neighborhood of Bedford-Stuyvesant. At the time, I was unaware that I was part of a new wave of young workers, college students, and artists (mostly trickling down from the Williamsburg and Fort Greene neighborhoods) seeking cheaper rent. "Bed-Stuy" was inexpensive, hyper-segregated, and bustling with informal street activity. Every day, I would hear solicitations from men selling "loose cigarettes," bootleg DVDs and CDs, and various t-shirts and apparel. There was a totem pole of hustlers—from the crack cocaine dealers who dominated the space in front of select bodegas, to the bootleggers, down to the crack users (one of whom tried to sell me two cans of tuna fish at 3:00 in the morning).

The hustler class was a fundamental part of Bed-Stuy's economy, rarely interrupted by New York's legal enforcers. Police would either be "two blocks too slow" to catch the bootleggers (who would lay their products on a bed sheet for an easy "scoop and run"), or they would simply pass by in quiet acceptance. Neighborhood residents were fully aware of who constituted the big (and most dangerous) players in the hustlers' economy. The average resident lived by the philosophy of "M.Y.O.B." (mind your own business), which, they hoped, would enable them to avoid being scathed by the affairs of others.

I became so intimately acquainted with the most felonious ranks of the hustlers' economy that I could easily compose a blueprint for all of the illegal businesses within walking distance of my apartment. Notably, the end of my block was an epicenter of crack cocaine activity. The corner bodega, owned by two Arab brothers, played host to the young crack dealers who dominated the sidewalk from midnight to 5:00 a.m. every night. Two doors down from the bodega, in a well-kept brownstone, were the kitchen and supply-center for the crack cocaine. Half a block away, a basement apartment hosted a prostitution circuit, mostly made up of crack-addicted females looking for ways to score in the wee hours of the night.

Once users would "cop" the drug by the bodega, they would spill farther down the street in front of the apartment hosting the prostitution ring, where they could use the drug as currency for sex. Others would consume the drug underneath scaffolding intended for the construction of a nearby school.

I had befriended the resident "muscle" of the prostitution ring, as he lived two doors from me, and we shared a common goal: "keep the crackheads away from my door." He preferred that his customers and his prostitutes not consume the drug near his property. I preferred the same. There were many nights when we would find each other outside at the same time—he armed with a metal pipe, and me armed with reason—attempting to "shoo away" the crackheads. In most cases, the pipe was more effective.

One cold February morning in 2004, an abandoned brownstone—recently purchased by a well-to-do couple—had been burned to the ground by exiting squatters, making my street more attractive to drug users. The city immediately erected scaffolding to repair the building. Scaffolding formed a perfect shelter from light, rain, and the eyes of passersby in the middle of the night. Consumers of crack could hide in the shadows without fear of being spotted by police. The hustlers preferred the crackheads to move far away from the bodega, only to return if they needed to make a purchase. Neighborhood residents were powerless to stop this vicious cycle, as NYPD required a 9-1-1 caller to face the alleged criminal *before* an arrest was made. Thus, the vast majority chose M.Y.O.B.

Although many would consider drug dealing to be "low class" and "dirty," it did provide those at the bottom with real power over a community. Hustling is essentially "a man's game" whereby men can assert themselves under older versions of patriarchal masculinity. With Bed-Stuy's limited opportunity structure, traditional patriarchal expressions of masculine dominance were limited to violence and illegal means of obtaining wealth. Mass incarceration, joblessness, and men's diminishing role in the available service economy, according to Phillipe Bourgois (1996), can feel like "an assault on (one's) masculine dignity."[1] Hustling can make an uneducated working-class man "feel like a man" again, as he can assert his *violent capital* over other community members.

As is seen in popular media representations of urban criminal underworlds, the drug trade promises wealth, women, and, most importantly, social status amongst one's peers. In a society in which status stratification[2] is an inevitable byproduct of capitalist desire, one can turn others' fear of violence into fast wealth, and as a result, earn street respect. In New York's deprived dozen, the use of violent capital (or the ability to make good on threats if necessary) has become the norm among certain young boys. The most impoverished neighborhoods in New York are either majority Black or Latino or a combination of both, and a particular type of masculinity has come to define what it means to be a young boy of color growing up in one of these neighborhoods.

The need for the expression of masculinity in Black and Latino neighborhoods is often overlooked in the study of juvenile delinquency. Many talk about the racial disparity in our prison systems, but equally as disconcerting is the gender disparity. Young boys represent 92 percent of all youth detainees. This is more of a reflection of the struggle with twenty-first century cultural identity than of any biological differences between men and women. When legitimate means of success are off the table, men typically seek the more attainable rewards generated from what bell hooks (2004) calls "imperialist, white-supremacist capitalist patriarchy."[3] The pressure to "act like a man" means more than just paying family bills and has more detrimental implications on one's future than simply physically defending oneself. For adolescent boys of color, living up to traditional expectations of manhood has the potential to result in life imprisonment.

Masculinity and the Construction of Black Identity

Notions of masculinity typically arise in the context of one's culture. Sociology has many definitions for culture; however, most scholars would agree that culture is a learned set of strategies or "a storehouse of pooled learning,"[4] as Clyde Kluckholn (1945) would say. These strategies become socially useful in a given environment. One's individual identity comes from the buffet served to us by culture. We as individuals simply choose to fill our plates with what we believe we *have to* eat. The buffet in New York City is large. Behavioral expectations are already provided for gays, straights, liberals, conservatives, Blacks, Whites, Brooklynites, Manhattanites, etc. We all pass over some items and fill our plates with others.

For young boys in the deprived dozen, the local culture in their neighborhoods are provided by the expectations of race, poverty, media interpretations of race and poverty (which expect criminal behavior from certain groups) and the legacy of their neighborhoods.[5] Black masculinity in a majority White society has been constructed over four centuries. The perception that African Americans[6] "act a certain way" is built on self-perpetuating stereotypical assumptions about Black manhood and is most acute among adolescent boys wrestling to discover their own identity. In her study of self-segregation in U.S. schools, Beverly Daniel Tatem (1997) claims that young boys following the expectations of Black masculinity are not choosing stereotypical "black posturing" because of racial assumptions alone; rather, theirs is a choice compelled by bridging the maturity gap between childhood and adulthood in adolescence. "As children enter adolescence, they begin to explore the question of identity, asking 'Who am I? Who can I be?' in ways they have not done before. For Black youth, asking 'Who am I?' includes thinking about 'Who am I ethnically and/or racially? What does it mean to be Black?'"[7]

What it means to be "Black in America" has had a major influence on the entertainment industry and has been studied by many scholars. As noted by Robert Staples (1982), "It is difficult to think of a more controversial role in American society than that of the black male . . . His cultural image is usually one of several types: the sexual superstud, the athlete, and the rapacious criminal."[8] In general, scholars would agree that Black Masculinity typically includes a magnified sexual appetite, a penchant for violent dominance, hostility towards homosexuality, and a cool attitude in the face of economic or intellectual inferiority. These stereotypes are both advantageous and disadvantageous to social mobility for African American males.

Black men simultaneously represent the most feared *and* desired category of manhood in U.S. society (some could argue the world), a result of the potency of resistance to centuries of social abrogation. As explained by Richard Majors and Janet Billson (1992), "Denied access to mainstream avenues of success, they have created their own voice. Unique patterns of speech, walk, and demeanor express the cool pose. This strategic style allows the black male to tip society's imbalanced scales in his favor."[9] What Majors and Billson call the "cool pose" allows a person with no physical capital to possess a form of cultural capital. Especially in the U.S. entertainment industry, African Americans have historically been the architects of new styles of dress, attitudes, and slang.

America's fascination with Black forms of expression began with the buffoonery seen in minstrel shows, which played on the worst stereotypes of African American slaves and became the most popular form of entertainment in the post-bellum 1870s. Although notions of "Africans savages" date back to seventeenth century tales of European exploration of Africa, the Black stereotypes that remain today have their roots in the fear perpetuated during the Reconstruction Era of the United States. The most popular vaudeville acts in the late nineteenth century included the decades-old characters of "Jim Crow," "Mr. Tambo," and "Zip Coon," who embodied the perceived intellectual inferiority, laziness, and gluttony of African American slaves.[10] White audiences of vaudeville and minstrel shows preferred the non-threatening characterizations of African Americans over the informal stereotypes of the dangerous ones.

As working class White Americans were adjusting to Reconstruction Era America after slavery, many promoted the stereotype of the violent/rapacious Black male in order to justify the solidification of legal segregation in the 1890s. For centuries, Black men were equated with animals: physically strong, sexually unrestrained, and intellectually inferior. Further, as African Americans attempted to position themselves in the industrial economy at the end of the nineteenth century, tales of Black criminality began to grow exponentially. Backed by the scientific community at the height of the Social Darwinist Era, many believed that the evolution of the African male was headed toward sexual barbarism. As noted by Arthur Saint-Aubin (2002), "whereas superiority was to be linked to skull size and intelligence, inferiority was to be linked to sexuality."[11] The myth of the "Black rapist" fed the American psyche and still feeds notions of Black male sexual hypersexuality to this day. Many of the Black Codes (laws in the American South solely directed at African Americans) between 1890 and 1960 made it illegal for African American men and White women to have any physical contact.

As the myth of the hypersexual Black male grew throughout the twentieth century, many African American men began to embrace it, and much of U.S. society slowly began to grow a curiosity for it. Record companies during the

Jazz and Rock 'n' Roll eras sought African American artists that were "cool and safe," but often audiences still found them to be "mysterious and dangerous." According to bell hooks:

> By the end of the seventies the feared yet desired black male body had become as objectified as it was during slavery, only a seemingly positive twist had been added to the racist sexist objectification: the black male body had become the site for the personification of everyone's desire . . . Many black males are simply acquiescing, playing the role of sexual minstrel.[12]

Because White audiences like a "taste of the exotic," many African American men still take advantage of these stereotypes. As noted by Staples, "A review of the record of white beliefs about black sexuality casts in bold relief the view that 'for the majority of white men, the Negro represents the sexual instinct in its raw state.'" Obsession with Black male genitalia dates as far back as the writings of Aristotle[13] and continue to bolster conceptions of Black male sexuality today.

Of all the Black male stereotypes created over the last one hundred and fifty years, that of the violent criminal has been methodically cultivated, commodified, and then outright embraced by U.S. society. In the 1960s, Black masculinity evolved into the reclaiming or forceful taking of political power, and notions of the "good Negro" (or obedient/deferential Negro) were purposefully destroyed and replaced with a more defiant/revolutionary representation. The 1960s and 1970s played a pivotal role in the creation of this violent male identity. Specifically, the combination of the media's portrayal of the antagonistic Black Power movement and record crime rates in African American neighborhoods created feared images of African American men.

Government forces—in particular the Federal Bureau of Investigation—found this "representation" to be too threatening to national security, therefore, most Black Power organizations were purposefully dismantled in the 1970s while economic forces drove Black neighborhoods deeper into poverty. The destruction of Black leadership combined with depression-level conditions in poor neighborhoods left a void in poor Black male identity that would later be filled (for some) with narcissistic self-preservation and violent undertakings. As was noted in the HBO documentary film *Bastards of the Party* (2005), "Out of the ashes of the Black Panther Party came gangs. Crips, Bloods, etc."[14] As Christopher Lasch (1979) would argue, in the wake of a failing economy, U.S. culture in general was turning toward selfish pursuits. Many Americans believed that "political solutions don't work"[15] therefore, they took charge of their pursuit of personal gain.

The use of violence, as it is connected to Black male identity, became the norm for the protection of one's person and property for poor urban men in the 1980s and 1990s. Violent capital is not useful for all African American men, but American patriarchal norms encourage men to seek some form of dominance over others. Whether it is sexual, economic, or physical dominance, when all other forms of dominance are limited, manhood often calls for the expression of power, even if that power is gained through violence. According to Major and Billson, "violence [at the end of the twentieth century] has become a readily available and seemingly realistic tool for achieving these critical social rewards; it is in this sense that violence can even become a form of achievement when everything else has failed."[16] Violent crimes in poor African American neighborhoods—which reached an all-time high in the 1990s—were considered a normal expression of manhood.

Race versus Class

Although institutional racism created many of the stereotypes for Black male identity, current socioeconomic forces push certain segments of the African American male population toward the stereotypes of the past. While we might view Black masculinity as purely a racial phenomenon, violence, homophobia, hypersexuality, and criminality are more closely linked to class than one's racial designation. Even though there is a significant racial disparity between African Americans and Whites in the prison population,[17] a more predictable indicator of prison entry across racial boundaries is that of poverty.

The masculine traits mentioned above tend to be more pronounced as one descends the economic ladder. Because young Puerto Rican men—who have been raised with generations of "machismo" sentiment—are in the same class situation as African Americans in New York City, these men have similar patriarchal behavioral expectations. A large proportion of New York's African American population migrated to the city in the 1940s and 1950s, and "those same years also saw a massive movement of people from Puerto Rico to New York."[18] Since that time, working-class African Americans and Puerto Ricans have settled in and around the same areas in the Bronx and Brooklyn, which has led to similar class situations, structural conditions, and even similar discrimination inflicted by other New Yorkers. New York City may be the only city in the United States in which African Americans and Latinos look at each other as one and the same.

As was argued by William J. Wilson (1978), due to the strides made during the civil rights era, African Americans are experiencing unprecedented amounts of success, and "class has become more important than race in determining black access to privilege and power."[19] Although the racial disparity in New York's prison system is one of the worst in the country, with close to 95 percent of all new youth detainees being Black or Latino,[20] a larger percentage of New York's detainees come from poor backgrounds. For young boys in the deprived dozen (whether Black or Latino), violent capital is more pronounced as a tool for gaining status among their peers. We may be blind to our classist tendencies in the United States; but, whether consciously or unconsciously, we propagate certain cultural expectations for each social class, which are commonly reflected in popular movies, music, and other forms of entertainment.

Hip Hop Culture

Within the context of U.S. pop culture, violence, homophobia, and hypersexuality—though considered by many to be undesirable—are a fashionable commodity for many young boys. Old modes of patriarchal domination are being bought and sold in mainstream Hip Hop, *gangsta* films, and even primetime television programming. Even though early twentieth century United States witnessed poor urban ghetto conditions through the work of 1960s' journalists, the cultural attributes of what many consider to be "ghetto" were not celebrated until the 1970s, as was seen in Black exploitation films. Black gangsta culture was born out of small films such as *Superfly* (1972) and *The Mack* (1973) but they were typically not viewed outside of Black audiences. When African Americans were searching for a new identity in the 1970s and 1980s, these films offered a new direction.

Hip Hop music was developing around the same time and came out of the disco party scene of the 1970s. Although most Hip Hop artists came from some the most dangerous neighborhoods in New York City, the majority chose not to focus on these conditions in the music and instead focused on the dynamics of the party scene. As rapping became more popular in the 1980s, some artists focused more on what would eventually be called *message music.* Rappers such as Chuck D (of Public Enemy) and KRS-ONE (of Boogie Down Productions) borrowed heavily from the militancy of the Black Power movement of the 1960s and preached Black pride, self-education, and general mistrust of conservative government politics. Many credit these artists with being positive role models for young boys in search of identity, but they only appealed to young Blacks and Latinos.

Hip Hop's "golden age" (1984-1993) offered many forms of dance music, love songs, and "conscious records," as many Rap artists spoke out against the urban decay experienced on a local level. White audiences were mostly disinterested in this new form of urban music until 1989. With the release of N.W.A.'s (Niggas With Attitude) *Straight Outta Compton,* record companies took notice of the young suburban thirst for this radically different type of Hip Hop music. There was something about the nihilistic and violent tales offered by N.W.A. that appealed to young White male audiences. Although some record labels—such as Def Jam Records—were experiencing commercial success in the 1980s, it wasn't until Gangsta gained popularity in the 1990s that Hip Hop became commercially viable. Thus began the nationwide commodification of gangsta culture.

To argue that Gangsta Rap has an effect on adolescent behavior is to understand Albert Bandura's (1977) concept of "social learning." According to Bandura, "Most human behavior is learned observationally through modeling: from observing others one forms an idea of how new behaviors are performed, and on later occasions this coded information serves as a guide for action."[21] Role models for young men come from family and neighborhood figures, or, in the case of young boys who have neither of these, from images portrayed in the media. For young Black and Latino boys, the bulk of male images come from Hip Hop culture.

With the onset of Gangsta Rap in the early 1990s, the dynamic of Hip Hop culture shifted away from the variety of "golden age" genres to this more violent form of music. Hip Hop artists did not see much success until they began to attract a large White audience. Such breakthrough albums as Dr. Dre's *The Chronic* (1992, EMI Distribution) were a hit among White youth. Even though rappers continued to talk about the dangerous conditions of urban ghettos, White youth could relate to the endangered aspects of U.S. patriarchal culture: love of money, dominance over women, and violence as a respected means to an end. Outside of Hip Hop, American pop culture in the 1990s preached equality for women, sensitivity for men, and tolerance for all forms of race, color, and sexual orientation. In a peak era of political correctness and multi-culturalism, Gangsta Rap offered an opportunity for young boys to experience the more classical attributes of patriarchal masculinity.

In the 1990s, Hip Hop's definition of Black manhood began to narrow. In her book *Hip Hop Wars,* Tricia Rose stated, "Since the mid to late 1990s, the social, artistic, and political significance of figures like the gangsta and street hustler substantially devolved into apolitical, simple-minded, almost comic stereotypes."[22] Moving away from the ideals of the Black Power movement of the 1960s—and instead borrowing from the legends of early twentieth century Italian-American gangsters—Gangsta rappers created a hybrid of nineteenth century patriarchal masculinity and the party music of the 1970s and 1980s: "The Gangsta Party." One of the first of his kind, Snoop Dogg preached the new ethos in one of his first hits, *Gin and Juice* (1993). In the song, Snoop Dogg pays respect to the "gangstas" present at the party, while lowering the status of all the women to mere sex objects ("Gs up, hoes down"). Whereas golden era Hip Hop viewed men and women as equals, Rap artists felt that, to be successful, they had to break with notions of gender equality.

Gangsta Rap preached the requisite use of violent capital as a means of maintaining masculine domination. For example, the New York City based Hip Hop group Mobb Deep emphasized one's ability to use violence, and not just talk about it, in their hit single *Shook Ones part II* (1995). In this song, Mobb Deep spoke directly to other Rap artists whom they believed were "fake criminals." The use of violence—particularly with handguns—became necessary for street credibility and subsequent entrance into the Hip Hop industry. This also solidified the use of violence as a singular path to manhood for working poor young boys.

For the young male audience who could most relate to Rap artists, Gangsta Rap created a template for manhood. Sexual dominance over women, get-rich-quick schemes, and the willingness to use violence to protect one's reputation became the foundation for underclass male identity. Ironically, women in Hip Hop were portrayed as shallow and devoid of personality, which may have contributed to the success-gap between young African American women and young

African American men. Women were able to create their own notions of womanhood, while young boys in urban ghettos could not be as creative.

The defiant attitudes of the 1960s' Black Power movement and the 1980s' conscious Hip Hop were turned into defiance against legal codes throughout the 1990s. Suddenly, the most negative stereotypes of what was considered to be "ghetto" were being celebrated by "keeping it real." As stated by Cora Daniels in her book *Ghetto Nation* (2007), "An argument could be made that this pride, this embracing of everything we are, the good as well as the bad, is somehow an aggressive way to erase feeling marginalized, which in the end can be an empowering act."[23] We have come to commercialize "ghetto," which has resulted in new fashions and has contributed to the "cool" Black posturing, but it has negative consequences in real urban ghettos.

Thus, the question of whether Hip Hop music causes violence, in general, and whether it contributed to the peak era of juvenile crime throughout the 1990s, in particular, has to be addressed. Proponents of the "life imitates art" argument would claim that Gangsta Rap directly causes juvenile crime rates. According to Rose, "The criticism that hip hop advocates and thus causes violence relies on the unsubstantiated but widely held belief that listening to violent stories or consuming violent images *directly* encourages violent behavior."[24] This is like suggesting that alcohol causes bar fights or that pornography causes rape.[25] To say that music has *that* much power over an individual's free will is to take an extreme stance on social learning theory. But to recognize that the music does have a major *influence* is to recognize that Hip Hop artists do create a template for manhood.

As we have entered an era in which we have successfully "commercialize(d) manufacturing of ghetto street life,"[26] we begin to wonder whether young people recognize the characters in Hip Hop as fictional characters. When I was a young boy growing up in the 1980s, I understood that "Rambo" was a character and that Sylvester Stallone was an actor. Therefore, I didn't readily tie a red bandanna around my head and try to shoot up my neighbors. But do young boys understand that "50 Cent" is a character based on the real Curtis Jackson (50 Cent's birth name)?

Hip Hop music videos today play on this thin line between fiction and reality, as is seen in 50 Cent's *Many Men* (2003) video. At this beginning of the video, credits are shown as if the audience is about to view a preview for a film preapproved by the American Motion Picture Association. The bottom of the screens reads: "G-Unit: Doesn't Get Any Realer." Featured in the video is the actor Mekhi Phifer playing the role of a cold-hearted gangster, and 50 Cent (playing himself) as a redeemed victim of the gangsta lifestyle. We, as the audience, understand that Mekhi Phifer is just acting, but do we understand that Curtis Jackson is doing the same?

The "keeping it real" culture that surfaced in the 1990s requires that all of 50 Cent's stories be true. This is assumed for all Hip Hop artists, which is why a White artist such as Enimem was able to have a great amount commercial success. His tales of dealing with a violent urban Detroit "checked out." A record of "keeping it real" has become a requisite for the survival of young males in ghettos, which may partially explain why so many young boys are turning to a life of crime even thought they could opt to struggle in the legitimate work world.

The Magnetism of Street Life

Several years ago, I conducted an interview with a young man who had recently been released by the New York State Department of Corrections. He was paroled after serving 85 percent of a five-year sentence for grand larceny auto theft. We were sitting in his mother's apartment in the East New York neighborhood of Brooklyn. I had asked him about his future plans. Looking out the tenth-story window of his bedroom, a sullen look came over his face. "Well, my P.O. [parole officer] wants me to get a job within the next two weeks, but the D.O.C. [Department of Corrections] froze my social security number, so I can't find a job. There is some work available at the McDonald's down the street, but I don't know if they'll take my application . . . And I don't know if I can work for $5 an hour."

He glanced over at me. "You know, I used to make ten grand [$10,000] a week boosting cars. I could get whatever I wanted with that money, and I only needed to lift like three cars a week." He stared out the window again, seemingly taking in the scene outside his window. "I think I'm going to get violated no matter what." He paused and then cringed. "You know, I think I'm gonna steal a few more cars, bank like twenty Gs, and then turn myself in. You know, so when I finish off the sentence, I'll have that money waiting for me when I get out." In his mind, he had choices, yet all of them seemed to point in the direction of continued imprisonment. For many young boys in the deprived dozen, the rewards of a criminal lifestyle far outweigh the risks.

The young man whom I engaged in an interview saw street life as his only viable option. Ethical concerns aside, the consequences for getting caught for this lifestyle are great. The criminal justice system was designed to make the average youth afraid to go to prison. But for young boys growing up surrounded by street hustlers—and who consequently find themselves involved with the criminal justice system—street life may be more *ordinary* than working a nine-to-five job.

Encouragement to be involved in criminal activities seems to come from all over, whether it's from the diminished expectations of society or the social pressure of local peer groups. According to Elijah Anderson (1994):

> For these young people the standards of the street code are the only game in town. The extent to which some children—particularly those who through upbringing have become most alienated and those lacking in strong conventional social support—experience, feel, and internalize racist rejection and contempt from mainstream society may strongly encourage them to express contempt for the more conventional society in turn.[27]

Street life possesses components of both "push" and "pull." The "push" comes from mainstream society, which openly accepts police profiling of young African American and Latino males if they wear anything resembling gang paraphernalia or resist the status quo. The "pull" comes from street life itself, which seems to guarantee immediate social rewards amongst one's peers. From a young age, boys of color are taught that they have been marginalized for centuries and that there is no reason for them to believe that this marginalization has ended. The "push" also comes from mainstream media such as the nightly news, music, or movies, which tell young boys, "You actually *are* a criminal, and this is all that we expect from you."

A common sense reaction to this upbringing is to forgo a legitimate world that will not accept them and to commit crimes as an act of defiance. Anderson calls this behavior "oppositional culture." Robert Merton (1938) would call this retreatism, while Mitch Duneier (1999) calls this the "fuck it! mentality," which is an "extreme form of retreatism, rather than a form of resignation."[28] In this case, it is a form of retreatism *away* from mainstream society and *toward* a more accepting criminal subculture, something that has a strong magnetic quality to it.

The "pull," strangely enough, comes simultaneously from one's peers and the *hidden values* of mainstream culture, which has commodified deviant behaviors. For young people in general, "cool" is often measured by one's willingness to engage in delinquency. This is even true of middle class kids. Cora Daniels wonders, "Why does ghetto have such pull? Why would kids going to a school rich enough to give them laptops still feel the need to thug it out on the corner or pull a knife on a classmate?"[29] Even among middle-class adolescents, seemingly nonsensical acts of violence occur with unexpected frequency.

Take, for example, the young boys in Garden City, New York (a wealthy suburb of New York City) who, on one warm June night in 2009, decided to act out the then-famous video game *Grand Theft Auto IV*. Ranging in ages from fourteen to eighteen, these six boys walked the streets of Garden City and committed acts of assault, robbery, burglary, menacing, and two attempted auto thefts. When they were caught and asked why they did it, then simply said that they were "bored."[30] These boys were from typical middle-class homes that had stable family structures. They were not intoxicated or high on drugs. Analysts and politicians alike jumped to blame the video game and violent music, while none considered the social rewards the boys could gain amongst their peers. As it turned out, these boys were unpopular at their respective schools and were seeking to obtain status.

For young boys in lower economic strata, the pressure to be delinquent is strong. In a series of interviews with a group of teens from New York City in 2006, I asked several respondents about manhood and what it means. Felix—a seventeen-year-old from the Bronx—explained, "On the block, it's about money. Selling. It's the easiest thing to do. . . . Guys function on envy. Who's doing what? Who's got the flyest girl? Who's got the nicest car?" Going to school and getting a legitimate job is a slow path to these social rewards, while the criminal trades offer the quickest and easiest route. Malik—a sixteen-year-old from Harlem—explained that, even if they don't want to, "men in certain neighborhoods are pressured into selling drugs, robberies, staying on the corner [loitering] . . . Doing dumb stuff! . . . Some guys try to put you down for knowing more than them." Both Felix and Malik stated that academic success did not accord much status.

Throughout the interviews, these boys had internalized old working-class notions of manhood. They stated that a man "commands respect" or that "a man has a legit job" and "a man is able to take care of his family." Some, like LeSean (age sixteen), were able to combine these older values with the newer ethos of Hip Hop culture. He stated, "Jay-Z, he's a real man. He's got money. He knows how to invest it. . . . He's a good role model. He influences people how to get money. And he also helps out the community." Even NBA Superstar LeBron James looks up to Jay-Z because he first made money in the drug trade, then made money from Hip Hop music, and then became one of the wealthiest African American investors in this country.

Most of these boys saw money as the means to all other social ends. They believed that, if you possess large amounts of money, society rewards you in kind: you get the girls; you get the respect; you get nice things. If the average drug dealer can make $5,000 a week,[31] and the average car thief can make $10,000 a week, some see these behaviors as worth the use of violent capital, even if it goes against their principles. The magnetism of unforeseen amounts of cash and the insulation provided by street respect is too great to deny.

Criminal justice officials should not only be using fear of imprisonment as a deterrent to crime, they also should be looking at these cultural components as complicit in the causes of crime. Thus far, crime control institutions have gone the way of subtracting the criminal element rather than adding a more stable structure to prevent the crime in the first place. An increasing number of community organizations are looking to replace these criminal codes for young boys with crime-free alternatives, and, in many instances, they are starting to have an impact.

Notes

1. Bourgois, Philippe. *In Search of Respect: Selling Crack in El Barrio.* New York: Cambridge University Press, 1996.

2. Weber, Max. "Class, Status, Party." [Ed.] Gerth and Mills: *From Max Weber: Essays in Sociology.* New York: Oxford University Press, 1946.

3. hooks, bell. *We Real Cool: Black Men and Masculinity.* (New York and London: Routledge, 2004).

4. Kluckholn, Clyde. *Mirror for Man: The Relation of Anthropology to Modern Life.* Phoenix, Ariz.: University of Arizona Press, 1985.

5. Even labeling their neighborhoods as a part of the *deprived dozen* might add more street credibility to individual boys from that neighborhood, and therefore, beef up their crime-related expectations.

6. The term "African American" in this chapter is used to describe any resident of the United States with African ancestry. The term "Black" is used to describe the cultural attributes of African Americans.

7. Tatum, Beverly Daniel. *Why Are All the Black Kids Sitting Together in the Cafeteria?* New York: Basic Books, 1997.

8. Staples, Robert. *Black Masculinity: The Black Male's Role in American Society.* San Francisco, Calif.: The Black Scholar Press, 1982.

9. Majors, Richard and Janet Mancini Billson. *Cool Pose: The Dilemmas of Black Manhood in America.* New York: Lexington Books, 1992.

10. Green, Alan W.C. "'Jim Crow,' 'Zip Coon': The Northern Origins of Negro Minstrelsy." *The Massachusetts Review, Vol. 11, No. 2.* (385-397), 1970.

11. Saint-Aubin, Arthur F. "A Grammar of Black Masculinity: A Body of Science." *The Journal of Men's Studies* (March 22, 2002).

12. hooks, p. 78.

13. Schiebinger, L. *Nature's Body: Gender in the Making of Modern Science.* Boston: Beacon Press, 1993.

14. Sloan, Cle (Director). *Bastards of the Party.* HBO Documentary Films, 2006.

15. Lasch, Christopher. *The Culture of Narcissism: American Life in an Age of Diminishing Expectations.* New York: W.W. Norton Company, 1979.

16. Majors and Billson, p. 33.

17. African Americans represent approximately 40 percent of the prison population, compared to their 12 percent share of the general population in the United States.

18. Freeman, Joshua B. *Working Class New York.* (New York: The Free Press, 2000).

19. Wilson, William Julius. *The Declining Significance of Race: Blacks and Changing American Institutions.* Chicago: University of Chicago Press, 1978.

20. Correctional Association of New York, The. "Juvenile Detention in New York City: An Annual Report: 2010." Retrieved July 16, 2010, from: http://www.correctionalassociation.org/publications/download/jjp/factsheets/detention_fact_sheet_2010.pdf

21. Bandura, Albert. *Social Learning Theory.* New York, N.Y.: General Learning Press, 1977.

22. Rose, Tricia. *The Hip Hop Wars: What We Talk About When We Talk About Hip Hop—And Why It Matters.* New York, N.Y.: Basic Books, 2008.

23. Daniels, Cora. *Ghetto Nation: A Journey Into the Land of the Bling and the Home of the Shameless.* New York, NY: Random House, Inc., 2007.

24. Rose, p. 9.

25. This was the main argument of Andrea Dworkin's book *Woman Hating* (1974).

26. Rose, p. xi.

27. Anderson, Elijah. "The Code of the Streets." *The Atlantic Monthly,* vol. 273, no. 5, 1994, pp. 81-94.

28. Duneier, Mitchell. *Sidewalk.* New York, N.Y.: FSG Books, 1999.

29. Daniels, p. 164.

30. Crowley, Keiran. (2008, June 27). "Game Boy Havoc on LI: Teens Busted in 'Grand Theft Auto' Spree." *New York Post.* Retrieved from website: http://www.nypost.com/p/news/regional/item_sZtcRgsjGwMGQ8xNtWJSwI

31. Amsden, David. (2006, April 9). "The One-Man Drug Company." *New York Magazine.* Retrieved from http://nymag.com/news/features/16653/

Chapter 5: Community Justice and the Reconstruction of Social Capital

Public Safety and the Role of the Community

Quality of life in a community is essential for the prevention of crime. Like many who have written about the concept of community, this discussion goes beyond the physical boundaries of a neighborhood and explores the interconnectedness, shared experiences and common goals of neighborhood residents. Of particular concern is the role of young people in the building of community identity. Actively coexisting with one's neighbors is a powerful deterrent to crime as potential criminals are unlikely victimize those with whom they identify. Therefore, the construction of community is dependent upon an individual's sense of self as it relates to his/her environment.

A common goal of most community members is that of public safety. Some would argue that urban living has degraded the interconnectedness of community and drives many of us to detach from common identity. We live in an era of increased dependency on social institutions to provide us with clean streets, neighborhood development, and a crime-free environment. Our change in societal behavior can be easily linked to increases in police presence over the past three decades, and some of our subsequent expectations of police to handle all affairs relevant to deviance and crime. Some scholars (Carr, Napolitano & Keating 2007) note that urban residents in poor neighborhoods "have high levels of dissatisfaction with police" and choose not to call police officials at all, but most middle income communities see police presence as a representation of their tax dollars at work.[1]

In their book *The Community Justice Ideal* (1999), Todd Clear and David Karp define public safety as "the assurance that offender(s) will not cause . . . harm to community members."[2] As a culture, we have become more detached in protecting our own communities and instead choose M.Y.O.B. On one occasion in my current suburban neighborhood, I had to resist this detachment as a group of teenagers walked past my house and then sat on a guardrail at the end of the street to smoke marijuana. From past experience, I understood if they continued unmolested that they would eventually feel comfortable enough to use this area on a regular basis. My first impulse was to pick up the phone and call the police, but instead I walked outside and confronted them, "You guys can't do that *here*." A few of my neighbors slowly emerged from their homes, as if they had been watching as well. One by one, they took turns yelling as the teens escaped over a nearby fence. My neighbors and I looked at each other with surprise, as if some form of archaic empowerment had been dusted off and reinstated. I haven't seen those teenagers since.

Urban environments tend to be viewed through the lens of *Gesellschaft*[3] suggesting that all community ties have been severed by density, diversity and fast-paced living. *Gemeinschaft* is typically only thought of being akin to small rural communities "characterized by a strong identification with the community, emotionalism, traditionalism, and holistic conceptions of other members of the community."[4] University of Chicago scholar Louis Wirth (1938) theorized that city living makes little room for intimate contact with neighbors and community members.[5] As was suggested by Wirth, urbanism causes much of the crime and social decay in cities because of the increased option of anonymity and escape into spatial oblivion. What makes New York City unique is the forced interaction and spatial proximity of its residents. The density in turn increases the likelihood of being thrust into face-to-face interactions with one's neighbors.

Public safety depends on the sense of responsibility of its community members. As was said so eloquently by Jane Jacobs in her infamous *Death and Life of Great American Cities* (1961):

> The first thing to understand is that the public peace—the sidewalk and street peace—of cities is not kept primarily by the police, necessary as police are. It is kept primarily by an intricate, almost unconscious, network of voluntary controls and standards among the people themselves, and enforced by the people themselves.[6]

Good community and public safety requires an active interchanging of neighborhood residents and social institutions. Residents must invest in their neighborhoods as if they are part owners.

Familiarity with one's community requires learning its most useful normative behaviors. Elijah Anderson (1990) would refer to this strategy as being "streetwise."[7] "A streetwise person is one who understands "how to behave" in uncertain public places . . . (a) recognition that street life involves situations that require selective and individualized responses." Even in a "bad" neighborhood, a community can be built with local knowledge and cooperation. *Re*-building a negative space into a positive neighborhood requires that residents take responsibility for each other.

Collaboration between neighborhood residents and local community institutions in order to fight crime is often referred to as *community justice*. Historically, teenagers have been left out of these coactive efforts. In fact, adolescents are seen as the cause of many neighborhood problems and urban community members tend to exclude them from crime prevention efforts. Alternative-to-

Incarceration programs can act as a bridge between teens and the "old heads" in a neighborhood. Whereas many urban residents in disadvantaged neighborhoods may be skeptical about rehabilitating crime-engaged youth, the following efforts show how a village can truly be involved in raising and educating its own children. This chapter focuses on two community-based ATI programs, both of whom draw from the talents and labor of their community residents in order to increase public safety.

The South Bronx and the Community Circuit Model

Although only separated from Manhattan by less than five hundred feet, Mott Haven and the surrounding neighborhoods in the South Bronx feel like a different city. Emerging from the 5 train on Third Ave & 149th street, it's easy to forget that that New York City is one of the wealthiest cities in the world. The second-hand clothing on the kids and the un-kept hairdos reflect the acceptance of neglect. Old men guard the entrances to store fronts, seated on half-empty vegetable boxes, gushing tales of teenage conquest and dreams delayed by life's twists. Every building, every corner absorbs the surrounding troubles like an ocean of struggle has washed over the streets. From the brand name presence missing from the store fronts, to the cracked sidewalks, all are obligated to hustle for survival in this area.

There is an isolating ellipse that cages these streets in—protecting it from the rest of the city . . . or vice versa. Manhattan is a distant land; a vacation spot; a promise to a child that never materializes. Your average New Yorker would never know about Mott Haven, unless he happened to drive down 149th or bravely ascend from the nearby train stops. This formerly industrial forgotten space manufactures insulated thinking. Adolescents in the South Bronx are fully aware of how others view them. How they are expected to act. With the social conditions available to them—or lack thereof—sometimes it's best to just conform to these expectations. This conformity may push the crime up rates in this area.

I trekked into Mott Haven regularly over a three-year period to observe one of New York City's more successful ATI programs. Located in the heaviest commercial district in Mott Haven, the space provided to the BronxConnect Youth Program was moderately intimidating. The industrial feel to the foyer revealed bare cement floors. The rhythmic thumping of *Bachata* music and the pungent smell of feral cats could always be found permeating the walls from neighboring buildings. The non-profit game in the ATI world was often a fight over scraps of city, state and private funding, and therefore was often reflected in the allotted real estate. Upon my first visit to the program, I observed the meticulous strategizing necessary for dealing with neighborhood deprivation.

On this particular night, all of the young participants sat in a circle reading a one-page pamphlet which read, "Guess Who? See if you can guess which one of your mentors has______." As all the kids sat themselves, four adult mentors sat down in the designated "hot seats" each holding a handful of index cards. The purpose of the activity was to test how well each participant knew their own mentor, and also to learn some unimaginable facts about each.

Each mentor stood and asked a *guess who* question from the cards. The stories ranged from drug addiction to "runnin' wild in the streets," but the common theme of "adolescent troubles" threaded each of the stories. All but one of the mentors told embarrassing tales, while the eldest remained silent.

The kids began to get curious about "Pop"—who had recently become an ordained Baptist minister—because he had failed to share any of his own personal stories. Pop stood and tucked his button-up shirt into his dark brown slacks as he began to tell a tale about his time in the Vietnam War: "I had spent a few years fighting in Vietnam and had seen and done some bad things." The room began to quiet as one of the kids asked, "Pop, did you ever kill someone?" This seemed to catch him off-guard. Pop, normally tranquil and jovial, began to frown as the memories unexpectedly seeped back into his mind. "No," he said, but he still looked quite shaken. Clutching his note cards while slightly grimacing he began to elaborate, "You know, when you fire a gun, you learn about yourself. Not like out here in the streets when you just shooting at nothing. But when you learn to shoot for real, you learn about yourself. If I had gone back to Vietnam, I could have killed someone." He paused and exhaled the last of his thoughts, "Those were my dark days."

Most of the young boys in the program had an atypical amount of knowledge about handguns. As I attended on Thursday nights, I would overhear the boys swapping stories about "someone who had been shot on their block," or "shell casings found on the sidewalk on their way to school." At some point in their young lives they had to face the arduous crossroad: quietly sliding past these dangerous conditions in hopes that no one notices them, or embracing the crime-engaged lifestyle and fight for their respect. Most of the boys and girls in BronxConnect had chosen to embody the crime-engaged lifes, which inevitably accelerated them into the criminal justice system.

Those attending the program were fortunate enough to not have to serve a long-term prison sentence. BronxConnect provided services for youth in Bronx Supreme and Family Courts. Founded as a tutoring program in 1998, the majority of the participants were mandated to attend for twelve to eighteen months as part of a "conditional suspended sentence."

At the time of my research, the program director, Ruben Austria, claimed that BronxConnect had an 84 percent success rate of "completion without incarceration or further court involvement." The program provided many types of services to its clients including: court advocacy, case management, a mentoring initiative, employment training, anger management and conflict resolution training: skills typically not available in the criminal justice system, nor in deprived neighborhoods.

The mentoring initiative connected successful adult members of the South Bronx community to court-involved youth and served as a means of rebuilding the social capital that had been lost over the past couple of generations. I refer to this coupling of model adults with youth—and the subsequent networking that takes place—as the Community Circuit Model. As older residents provide mentoring and tools to their younger community members, they in essence are investing in their future public safety. Youth in the South Bronx are typically lacking in useful social networks that lead to viable job opportunities. As is said by Robert Putnam in *Bowling Alone* (2000), "One pervasive stratagem of ambitious job seekers is 'networking,' for most of us get our jobs because of whom we know, not what we know."[8] Mentoring combined with case management provides the youth with an enhanced network of community members plugged in to legitimate work, school, and community service opportunities.

The clients of BronxConnect have faced some of the worst conditions in New York City. Bronx County (the third poorest county in the United States in 2000[9]) tends to exhibit typical predicators of juvenile crime: high rates of poverty, poor secondary school achievement, and a deprived network of community members who have very low rates of high school completion and college attendance.[10] (See figure 5a.) BronxConnect, located in Mott Haven, serves as an institution of mobility in the least mobile neighborhood in New York City.

Poverty in an urban neighborhood is often exacerbated by the poor network of job marketability of its residents. "Whom one knows" truly matters in a global economy that demands increased specialization and competition. Social capital is not the sum total of job skills or acquired educational achievement, but rather *who* connects other individuals to these vital resources. Pierre Bourdieu (1986) defined social capital as "the aggregate of the actual or potential resources which are linked to the possession of a durable network of more or less institutionalized relationships of mutual acquaintance and recognition."[11]

Although many migrate to New York City seeking elite college education—or to compete in a demanding professional world—what often expedites actual professional mobility is a "good word" from a friend at work, a "letter of reference" from a renowned colleague, or a job position "held open" by a family member. If it could somehow be quantified, labor experts would likely find that mobility is near impossible without the assistance of acquaintances.

Although it may be banal to include "who you know" on one's resume, community networking is a soft skill that is just as necessary for mobility as any hard skill (such as computer training or a second language). As is said by Putnam, "Just as a screwdriver (physical capital) or a college education (human capital) can increase productivity (both individual and collective), so too social contacts affect the productivity of organizations and groups."[12]

Many economists and state/city officials see the problem of poverty as simply a matter of "taking personal responsibility" and diving head-long into the job market and the structure it provides. As was said by James Coleman in *Social Capital in the Creation of Human Capital* (1985), "Even in the new institutional economics, there is a failure to recognize the value of concrete personal relations and networks of relations—what [Granovetter, 1985] calls 'embeddedness'—in generating trust, in establishing expectations, and in creating and enforcing norms."[13]

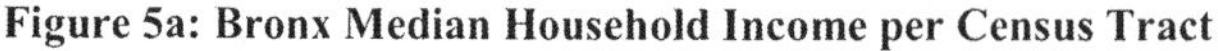

Figure 5a: Bronx Median Household Income per Census Tract

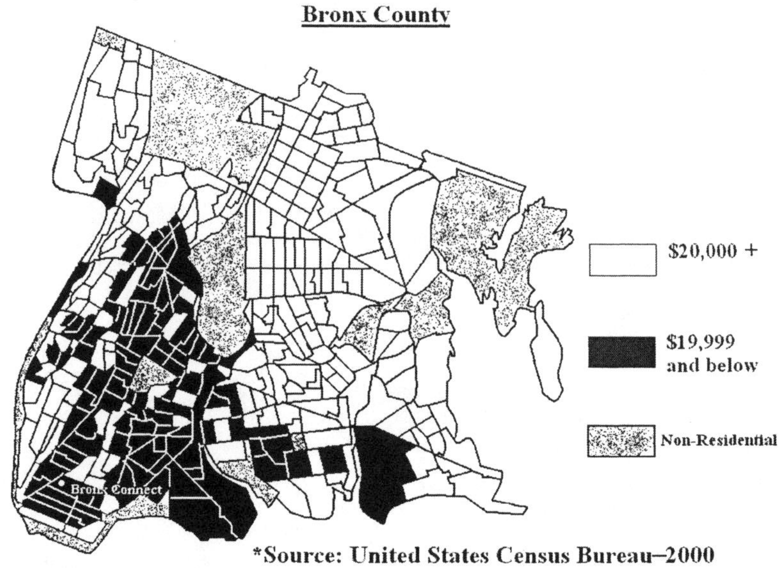

BronxConnect, through its mentoring initiative, attempted to bridge the divide between real marketability and deprived structural opportunity by piecing together a network of individuals with increased human capital. There was the recognition that assisting all of the community members has positive outcomes for all of its individuals. In an interview with BronxConnect Program Director, Ruben Austria, I asked, "Why do these kids deserve rehabilitation?" He promptly answered, "Number one: These are our kids. We know them outside of their cases. They're our sons, cousins, church members, etc. Number two: Because of the creativity and intelligence of the youth. We need to let them know that they are world trend setters. This is the next generation of leaders in community, for evil or for good." It is with these core values that BronxConnect tried to rehabilitate juvenile offenders.

The mission of the program was not simply to administer services, but also to create lasting relationships. By job description, the case managers at BronxConnect were there to provide the life skills training, individual counseling, and accurate reporting on the client's progress to the Supreme or Family Court judges. But, as Ruben would say, "what makes the program work is when they can advocate for their entrance into a certain school, or when they personally escort a kid to a job interview." This requires a good relationship and level of trust that most of the participants are reluctant to acquire.

On the Thursday's "activity nights," the case managers would collectively get together to plan the direction of the night. The themes tended to focus on "problem solving" or "conflict resolution." Besides the individual training the clients received on Tuesdays, the "life skills" training and religious ideology tended to be filtered into recreational activities.

Conflict resolution was often taught through the analysis of a particular story. On one June evening, Nicole, one of the case managers, began the group session by telling a story of a teenage girl who was raped at the age of 6, and then went on to fight this trauma to become a successful young adult. But the young girl eventually failed out of college because of perceived rumors of her promiscuity. Nicole then asked the group "Why did these rumors affect her?" This was an exercise intended to make the clients think about how people sometimes "justify failure" through past traumatic events.

Antonio—one of the participants—claimed that "abuse is a cycle. If someone is abused, they tend to abuse others or look to be abused." Antonio was only two weeks away from finishing the program and clearly reflected the critical thinking skills and values of the mentors and program staff. Cynthia—another client close to completing the program—reiterated, "Abuse sometimes can be addictive. Some people rely on it."

The participants took the assignment seriously, and found an opportunity to relate the young girl's story to their own situations. One of the mentors sealed the assignment with some final words, "The moral of the story here seems to be to not use your tragedy as a crutch. Just because you've dealt with some hardships in life, doesn't mean that you have the *right* to fail and do bad things." Through the direction of the case managers, mentors and participants alike were able to discuss issues that affect them on a daily basis and connect these experiences with strategies for dealing with future struggles.

Ruben explained that it took about six months for a good relationship between clients and case managers to develop. And in many cases the relationships were strong. In an interview with a former participant, I asked about her lasting relationships with BronxConnect and she replied, "Ruben and Doug were like fathers to me. My father died when I was three years old. Joanne (her case manger) was like a sister." The majority of the clients who made it to the six month mark tended to go on to successfully complete the program. At the end of twelve months, participants not only learned many soft skills for survival in their neighborhoods, but they internalized the codex of what had been taught.

Every six months, BronxConnect would hold a graduation ceremony for the participants that successfully completed the program. The community circuitry was evident as participants, parents, mentors and other community members could come and celebrate the capital that had been gained. At one ceremony in particular, there was ample evidence of the internalization of the values and skills learned in the program.

This ceremony was held on a hot July day in 2006. The room was filled with fidgety and gossiping teens, proud parents, blue and white balloons and streamers, and a whispering chorus of paper fans made from the program fliers. The room went quiet as the award ceremony began. Kim began her congratulations to the youth with a quote from the bible: "Proverbs 22:6: Train a child in the way he should go, and even when he is old he will not turn away from it." Her focus was on the future and the faith that her clients would lead a good lifestyle after their departure from the program.

With each award, an aloof youth—their facial expressions indicating exaggerated disinterest—would calmly stand to receive it. Shortly after the frame of the award touched their hands, disinterest instantly transformed into an inspired gleam. Applause was liberal—hoots and shouts often. Each person was involved with each award. One of the kids stood up after receiving his plaque and thanked *each* staff member for "looking out for me."

Cynthia—a client who had just completed her twelve-month cycle, and was on her way to probation and Youthful Offender[14] status—explained that without the program she would probably have gone "the opposite direction." Normally joking with the other clients, Cynthia paused with seriousness as she received her award for "excellence." Looking around the room, she smiled at her mentors and case manager and finally proclaimed, "Thank you for allowing me to prove myself and learn self-control."

In this moment, the transformation of someone who viewed the program solely as an extension of the court system, to someone who saw the staff at BronxConnect as familial, took shape. These types of relationships take time, patience, and effort, things that are rarely available inside of the juvenile justice system. The end goal of the program was to use the relationships with model community members to inspire and modify the behavior of the participants. Essentially, nothing was forced. The clients were given a set of mandates handed down from their respective judges, and then it was up to them to follow through. There were those who dropped out of the program and descended back into the criminal justice system; but for those who made it through to the end, the sense of trust and reciprocity that developed aided in the facilitation of a crime free lifestyle.

The Lower East Side and the Total Community Justice Model

On September 16, 1975, NYPD officers Andrew Glover and Frederick Reddy were making a routine traffic stop on East Fifth Street in the Lower East Side of Manhattan. A red convertible had been suspiciously pulled to the side of the street with its hazard lights flashing. The officers approached the car, and after a brief exchange of words, the driver was said to have shot and killed both police officers without provocation.[15] The assailant fled the scene and was never heard from again. The officers had only lived long enough to make it to nearby Bellevue Hospital.

Officer Glover was said to be a dedicated servant of the ninth precinct and a celebrated hero for the welfare of children in the Lower East Side. A year after his death, Glover became the inspiration and namesake of the Andrew Glover Youth Program. This ATI program was created to provide for the disadvantaged youth of lower Manhattan; youth who were seeing their opportunities dissolve with the numerous amounts of economic crises at the time.

Throughout the 1970s, the Lower East Side was a crime-ridden corner of lower Manhattan where few outsiders dared to venture. Today, this neighborhood is nearing a two decades long era of transition. Gentrification—fueled by the gold rush to grab any last bit of "cheap" Manhattan real estate—has transformed this neighborhood from a predominantly poor Latino neighborhood to a mixed income and mixed ethnic neighborhood. Wealthy college students intermingle with poorer families that have been there for generations. But in certain areas, crime is still a concern and social services are a necessity.

The day-reporting site of the Andrew Glover Youth Program reflects the mixed culture of the neighborhood. Outside, the dull crumbling brick is riddled in graffiti contrasting the sidewalk filled with empty food containers from a nearby Chinese restaurant. Inside, the center consists of two small conjoined rooms dividing an office-space, two mini-bathrooms, an open kitchen and a small recreation area. White walls are filled with the decorative touch of the program director. Framed black and white photographs of past participants neatly line the area surrounding the recreation table. Newspaper articles of past successes and program initiatives hang in the hallway, reminding the staff and the kids of what can be achieved. An ancient life-sized poster of Muhammed Ali taunting a TKO'ed Sonny Liston dominates the bathroom door. The poster's slogan, "Impossible is Nothing," speaks volumes to the dynamic of the program.

I chose a cool autumn evening in 2005 for my first visit to the program where I was introduced to the elder participants: Cesar and Cesar (no relation). Both were slightly overweight, but one was taller than the other. As I found a seat, they were occupied in front of a large screen television where they were bantering, laughing, and intensely engaged in a PlayStation game. Big Cesar began to add commentary to the virtual racing game while he waited his turn, "Y'all can't drive, please!" He proceeded to put a mix tape in a nearby radio. Amanda, the sole case manager on duty, warned them about the content, "Don't put on anything with any profanity." "Near impossible," I thought to myself considering the usual content of popular Hip Hop. Within seconds a thunderstorm of *mutha fuckas* and other various *disses* rained from the speakers as every kid in the room sang along. I asked what we were listening to. "G-Unit versus D-Block," exclaimed Little Cesar.

Soon after, Big Cesar sat down to play the racing game. Little Cesar began to criticize his driving skill, "Dude, you've never even drove before."

"Yo, I got a license! I'll put money on it!"

"Whatever."

The betting had begun: if Big Cesar could prove that he had a driver's license, then Little Cesar would owe him fifty dollars. Moments later, Amanda confirmed that Big Cesar indeed had a license, though the nature of payment seemed to fizzle within seconds.

Being a group of boys only, a predictable amount of emasculated teasing went on as the group swelled to seven people. Both Cesars did most of the talking and most of the homophobic remarks, frequently calling each other "faggot." With every battle rhyme on the radio, the volume would increase. Amanda would proceed to turn it down, but that would only last for a minute or so as a hand would sneak towards the volume button.

Then boys seemed to get noticeably more placid when Yassell arrived. A petite young Latina, Yassell was the only girl in the program. The boys mumbled amongst themselves as she removed her jacket and made it over to the recreational area. Cursing, banging, and loud chatter came to a minimum as she sat and joined in as "one of the guys."

Even though she was the lone case manager, Amanda seemed to fit right in with her clients. Dressed in a sweatpants and a sweatshirt—her arms wrapped around the shoulders of a client at any given moment—her physical contact with them appeared familial. She was the matriarch for the night and in charge of their activities. Day reporting centers tend to maintain a four-to-one client to staff ratio, but she was not intimidated.

Eventually, the numbers were too large to involve everyone in video games, so I was invited to play a game of "Spades." I sat at the long kitchen table nestled into the corner of the room, as the cards were being dealt between Little Cesar, Jose, Yassell, and myself. Big Cesar sat beside me and drew "tags" on a plain piece of paper for the remainder of the game. Jose, my partner, was quiet and tended to bet very high on each hand. Little Cesar and Yassell turned out to be a good. As this was my first exposure to them, I was hoping to establish some *cred* by playing the game well, but Jose and I continuously lost hand after hand. He was a little too confident. As Yassell quietly gained advantage in each hand, Little Cesar would banter. With each hand lost, he would rib me a little more, "You sure you know how to play this?" As the last hand played out, Amanda walked by and commented on Jose's strategy, "Oh you're playing with *Jose?* Did he over-bid every time?"

"Yup."

"Oh yeah, he's feeling himself too much."

Within seconds Amanda demanded a shift in activities, "Alright. It's time to clean up! It's time to put on the movie." In under a minute, the total compliance of the participants reached a paramount as chairs were pulled from all sides of the room to line up in front of the television.

This type of atmosphere allowed the participants to relax and relieve themselves of the pressures of the court system. All of them were court-involved, and all of them had prison sentences dangling over their heads if they failed the program. Like BronxConnect, the case managers of the Andrew Glover program acted simultaneously as court advocates, mentors, and counselors.

The Andrew Glover Youth Program was founded with three primary goals in mind: "1) Intervene and reclaim young people from the lives of crime, 2) Provide the overloaded court system with a reliable alternative to incarceration, 3) Make the Lower East Side and East Harlem communities safer for everyone."[16] Inspired by the death of Officer Glover in 1975, involvement with the community was the template for the program which encouraged active involvement in the criminal justice system. The program's intentions were to follow in Glover's footsteps by providing services to "at risk" youth.

The program director, Angel Rodriguez, was also raised in the Lower East Side and was content with his record of service to his own community. He claimed that the Andrew Glover Program only had a 9 percent recidivism rate (new conviction within three years) compared to the 64 percent produced by the sum total of all other "New York State programs." During our initial interview, I asked him how his program achieved such low recidivism rates compared to the prison system. "Because it's community-based," he said proudly. "The kids walk into the center and the counselors live in the community, therefore, it makes for more contact." Angel only hired case managers who lived in the Lower East Side (or near his second site in East Harlem). As a result, there was a guaranteed intimacy and vested interest from all the community members involved.

Like BronxConnect and most other ATI programs, Andrew Glover drew its clients from the juvenile parts in Manhattan Family and Supreme Court. They served youth between the ages of thirteen and twenty-one, but mostly provided services for adolescents. The clients had court-mandates and a reduced sentences contingent upon the successful completion of the program (which can range from three months to twelve months, depending on their "risk to the community"). Program activities ranged anywhere from health classes, to job preparation, or "street law" training seminars.

Because the staff and clients all reside in Lower East Side, I claim that the Andrew Glover Program employ a Total Community Justice Model. On the side of the staff, interest in public safety goes well beyond work satisfaction as successful clients translate to crime-free neighbors. As for the clients, failure in the program would also equal failure in the eyes of one's community members. The clients typically meet with their case managers/court advocates three nights a week, but could also run into them in the streets. For both parties this was a total community investment. Relationships were closer at Andrew Glover compared to other programs because the clients, essentially, "know" the program staff before they ever come into the program.

Total investment of community members in criminal justice affairs contributes to public safety and the overall quality of life in a community. Crime and deviant behavior in general are not only the result of a deprived structure, but also the deprived connections between community members. Putnam would even suggest that neighborly relations are "*more important* than a state's education level, rate of single-parent households, and income inequality in predicting the number of murders per capita."[17] Knowing one's neighbor can have an incredible impact on violent crime prevention.

Increased police presence in New York City since the early 1990s has led to a movement of moving *more* people off of the streets and into their homes, and therefore, creating less opportunity for community involvement. As was suggested by Jacobs (1961) the implied "danger" in New York City communities "make people fear the streets . . . And as they fear them, they use them less, which makes the streets still more unsafe."[18]

What is truly necessary for public safety, as Jacobs would suggest, is more "eyes on the street." Jacob's treatise to *urban gemeinschaft* was written about a neighborhood adjacent to the Lower East Side. Although crime rates in Greenwich Village during the 1960s were not significantly lower than the city as a whole, there was an appearance of safety and community involvement, what Robert Sampson would call "collective efficacy"[19]—or as Clear defines as "the ability of an aggregate to put shared expectations for their community into action and to achieve desired qualities of community life."[20] The hustle and bustle around 6th Ave and Washington Square Park provided more eyes, more witnesses, and therefore more people potentially invested in your safety.

Along with weakened social ties, the participants at Andrew Glover have to deal with the same structural deficits as other kids entering the criminal justice system. Like the clients of BronxConnect, participants at Andrew Glover are faced with poor conditions, but on a highly unusual scale considering the wealth surrounding the Lower East Side. Like much of the rest of the city, there is an odd correlation between race and poverty, and therefore, a lack of community resources. The Lower East Side in particular is representative of the pattern of "wealth on top of poverty" that has existed for decades in New York City. Manhattan (New York County) simultaneously has the some of the wealthiest and poorest zip codes in the United States. The Lower East Side is a poor community surrounded by wealth: an island within an island.

Including the Lower East Side, Latino communities in New York City tend to exhibit the worst opportunity structures. The median household income for Latinos in the city is the lowest amongst any racial group at $29,312. 71.5 percent of Latino children are born into poverty which one could argue leads to a disproportionate amount of representation in juvenile detention centers (30 percent).[21] These conditions, combined with the negative effects of concentrated incarceration, only make the youth in these neighborhoods more "at risk." As is said by Clear in his study of the effects of incarceration on social capital:

> When incarceration reaches a certain level in an area that already struggles for assets, the effects of imprisonment undermine the building block of social order. This is, for these neighborhoods, a kind of double whammy. First, they suffer the disruptions that occur when large numbers of residents are coercively removed and imprisoned. Then they struggle with the pressures that occur when large numbers of former convicts return to community life.[22]

Yet, the beam of hope for the Lower East Side is that the cultural values of most Hispanic immigrant communities tend to lend themselves to more family and community involvement. Contrary to a typical urban community, Latinos have a penchant for community activity as is evident in the number of people outside in most Latino neighborhoods. Public safety begins with strong community ties. The Andrew Glover Youth Program attempted to create a strong sense of "belonging" and "investment" through active involvement in the criminal justice system.

The case managers (or "Youthworkers") at Andrew Glover also double in their roles as court advocates. As case managers, they provided individual counseling, group activities and home visits where they are allowed to gain access to the client's home and family life. As court advocates, they serve as the link between the criminal justice system and local community interests. They are required by job description to be actively involved in the safety of their community, as is illustrated within the requirements advertised in an Andrew Glover Youth Program brochure:

> The Youthworker must live in the community
> The Youthworker must be available 24 hours a day, seven days a week
> The program must operate on streets where youth spend most of their time
> There must be constant moral counseling to make youth aware of the consequences of their behavior
> There must be continual contact and cooperation with the courts and legal and social service agencies.[23]

The Youthworker position is intense and requires a continued commitment. As clients are held to account, so are those who provide the services, which equals out to greater community investment. I had asked Amanda—a case manager *and* former client of Andrew Glover—about this total commitment, "Is it difficult to serve your community as a role model 24/7?"

"It's hard," Amanda explained. "For example, one Saturday I was invited to party at a club, but didn't go because I might see one of my clients! You have to put work before personal life. It becomes an everyday thing. From shopping, to laundry, on the bus. They make you stand straight and narrow. Although my personal life is compromised at times, it's worth what I get back from my community."

Amanda's story was unique and inspiring because of how she was turned around by the program. Like many of her clients, she was a troubled teen involved in criminal activities, gang affiliation, and eventually, the juvenile justice system. The attachment created by the program helped to turn her around. "I felt unloved. The counselors provided love. They gave a shit. Glover did it." As an active community member and mentor to her clients, Amanda served as a role model and constant reminder to her clients of the "right path."

Role-modeling was a key component to the success of the program. The preachings of those who had not experienced deprived conditions, would often fall on deaf ears. Andrew Glover often pooled from those who made something of themselves even though the chips were stacked against them. On one particular Wednesday night, the program invited a man who had recently finished a twelve-year prison sentence, but was dedicated to a crime-free lifestyle. Wednesday nights at Andrew Glover was typically for "health class" which usually covered health, hygiene, nutrition and sex education; though, the topics could spill into "street justice" or "housing concerns."

Daniel—a community member and ex-prisoner—had evidence of a hardened life written into his face. The rings under his eyes spoke volumes to the hard work he put in to reach his current position in life. Still wearing his uniform from the Doe Foundation, Inc., he spoke without censorship, "All young kids start the same. Everybody loves you when you're a baby. And then when you hit like twelve, thirteen, fourteen, you come to a fork in the road. You can do the good thing or the bad thing. . . . And that's when people need love and attention the most!"

Daniel openly confessed his past. He made it through high school, two years of college, and a few years as a Marine before he turned to street hustling. "I was waking up in the morning every day, going to work, and in a week I was making a few hundred dollars. Some of my mans was getting up late, and by the end of the day they was making Gs. So I said, *I got to get some of that.*" He turned to selling cocaine in his early twenties, neglecting his family and eventually ending up in prison for more than a decade.

As he spoke, most of the participants were engaged and listening, while some seemed disenchanted. Daniel wanted to emphasize that incarceration was not easy, "When you get in, either you become someone's bitch or you going to take a few lumps. Day in and day out. You can't win that game." He went into tales of being in isolation for twenty three hours a day, the bad food and the poor treatment from the guards. "But I can't blame them. I got myself there. They used to say, 'We didn't invite you here. You got yourself in here.'"

A major lesson of his talk was a hard pill for an average boisterous teen to swallow: "If you follow the rules, then things become a lot easier. If you don't follow the rules, then they got something for you!" Things that are often overlooked as teenagers, like choice in friends, were emphasized during his talk: "You shouldn't pledge allegiance to those who will only backstab you when the police come. You know the best way to get away from those dudes? Say wassup and then do this." He looked down at his wrist as if checking the time, "Oh damn, I'm late. I'll get with you later. And then bounce." Although a little "rough around the edges" with a "not-so model" history, Daniel still served as a good role model because he could relate to the daily tribulations of the clients in the program. He could reach them on a level that state officials, or anyone raised outside of that type of environment, could understand.

Like a "neighborhood watch" organization or a "block party association," Andrew Glover provided a wide net of community observation and involvement. Their success may partly be due to the unending line of informal social controls that the clients encounter on a regular basis. Clients may encounter their Youthworker at any given moment; or other neighbors may involve themselves after agreeing with the intentions of the program, providing more eyes for the control of deviant behavior. Compared to clients in other ATI programs, who only have to exhibit good behavior for the three or four hours that they see their case managers, participants in Andrew Glover have to make a lifestyle change because of the continuous supervision.

Moreover, successful role models in a community contribute to public safety more directly than criminologists have assumed. Imitation, especially in childhood, is where culture begins. We respond to our environment as actors seeking approval from those around us. If involvement in the criminal trades is "the norm" in a neighborhood (and if it is lucrative), then it would certainly be a rational choice for a community member to involve himself in the drug trade as a member of that community. If there is a strong working class ethos in a neighborhood, then young people will likely live by that code.

The type of school, court and family involvement of the staff at Andrew Glover tends to fill the gaps that our current legal system cannot fill. Where neighbors seek more involvement in the rehabilitation of a young community member, the criminal justice system has no forum. Where family members of court-involved need assistance, the criminal justice system cannot deliver. As was said by Angel Rodriguez, "It's important to understand their living situations to figure out their needs. Sometimes the kid is sleeping on the floor or in the living room and has no privacy. At other times parents have no control over them because of their situation. The criminal justice system tends to look at parents as failed architects of their kids, and don't utilize making alliances with them." This connection between family, victims, offenders, and community members is a positive step towards community justice.

Notes

1. Carr, P., Napolitano, L., and Keating, J. (2007). "We Never Call the Cops and Here is Why: A Qualitative Examination of Legal Cynicism in Three Philadelphia Neighborhoods." *Criminology, 45 (2),* pgs. 445-480.

2. Clear, Todd and David R. Karp. *The Community Justice Ideal: Preventing Crime and Achieving Justice.* Boudler, Colo.: Westview Press, 1999.

3. Tonnies, Ferdinand. *Gemeinschaft und Gesellschaft.* [Ed.] Charles P. Loomis. The Michigan State University Press, 1957.

4. Lyon, Larry. *The Community in Urban Society.* Long Grove, Ill.: Waveland Press, 1999.

5. Wirth, Louis. (1938) "Urbanism as Way of Life."*American Journal of Sociology, 44(1).*

6. Jacobs, Jane. *The Death and Life of Great American Cities.* New York: Random House, 1961.

7. Anderson, Elijah. *Streetwise: Race, Class, and Change in an Urban Community.* Chicago: University of Chicago Press, 1990.

8. Putnam, Robert. *Bowling Alone: The Collapse and Revival of American Community.* New York: Simon & Schuster Paperbacks, 2000.

9. According to the United States Census Bureau (2000).

10. According to the United States Census Bureau (2000), only 3.6 percent of the population of the neighborhood of Mott Haven has a college education.

11. Bourdieu, Pierre. "The Forms of Capital." J. Richardson [Ed]. *Handbook of Theory and Research for the Sociology of Education*. New York: Greenwood, 1986.

12. Putnam, p. 29.

13. Coleman, James S. (1988) "Social Capital in the Creation of Human Capital." *The American Journal of Sociology, 94.* pp. S95-S120.

14. In New York State, Youthful Offender status guarantees that a adolescent offender's record will be permanently sealed after the offender turns eighteen years old.

15. Hudson, Edward. (1975, September 17). "Two Policemen Are Slain; East Side Gunman Escapes." *New York Times,* p. A93.

16. The Andrew Glover Youth Program: "Transforming Lives" (brochure—2005).

17. Putnam, p. 309.

18. Jacobs, p. 107.

19. Sampson, R., Raudenbush, R., and Earls, F. (1997). "Neighborhoods and Violent Crime: A Multilevel Study of Collective Efficacy." *Science, 277.* pp. 918-924.

20. Clear, Todd. "The Problem with 'Addition by Subtraction': the Prison-Crime Relationship in Low Income Communities." Marc Mauer and Meda Chesney-Lind [Eds.] *Invisible Punishment.* New York: The New York Press, 2002.

21. A Citizens' Committee for Children Status Report: 2005

22. Clear, Todd, p. 183.

23. Andrew Glover Youth Program brochure: "There's a better way" (2005).

Chapter 6: Antonio's Story: Warfare and Redemption

Even though there are rehabilitative services available to adolescent boys in New York City, they are often not discovered until after they have had contact with the criminal justice system. Certainly a young man can escape a crime-free lifestyle with good family support, coactive relations with one's neighbors, constructive educational guidance, and strong personal will. But for many young boys in the deprived dozen, peer pressure, mainstream cultural goals, and economic forces tend to drive them towards street life.

Adolescent boys in impoverished neighborhoods are aware of their choices. They see examples of men that look just like them who have "put their heads down" and put in the hard work to become successful attorneys, wealthy athletes, or blue-collar workers. At some point—typically before entrance to high school—they are faced with the arduous crossroad. Some police and education officials are beginning to see middle school as the most volatile time. "Straight-A" students coming out of fifth grade are exposed to drugs, alcohol, and sexual exploits, and then they suddenly see their grades slip. Socio-metric rank amongst one's peers becomes more important than career trajectory, and this sometimes results in deviant choices.

Of all the young men that I have interviewed, none danced on both sides of the road more than a young man named Antonio. Born and raised in the Tremont section of the Bronx, Antonio saw violence and street hustling as a norm. He had walked both paths, and had the insight to distinguish between the two. A former client of BronxConnect, he had appreciated the tools that had been given to him, as he wanted to demonstrate in our conversation on a hot summer day in 2009.

I met with Antonio in his place of employment on Fordham Avenue, an area that he considered to be "the Manhattan of the Bronx." Taking a break from his job in a popular clothing store, he pulled me to an under-utilized corner. With a popular radio station blasting over the intercom speakers, he began to showcase his accomplishments. "I got my GED, if you want to go and make a Xerox of it." He pulled an eight-by-eleven inch sheet of manila paper from his jacket pocket. "Got it in May 2009. I went to school to do this, and I'm thinking of going to college but I'm waiting because I'm supposed to be receiving a scholarship from Nike; so I can work for them full-time."

Antonio was openly proud of his accomplishments; especially of his education. Lacking access to a photocopy machine, I pulled out my camera phone and snapped a photo of his GED diploma as he discussed his new found passion for retail sales. "I was talking with my boss about working here and being like the main person, and I was chosen. I am the most knowledgeable person in the sneaker department, shoes athletic wear, what's good for what. So I'm supposed to be promoted to working for Nike, so I'm waiting to see what happens with that before I go back to school. If anything I want to apply for school in December."

In the ATI world, Antonio would be the poster-child for success. Originally charged with aggravated assault (a class B Felony), he had successfully completed his court-mandated obligations to a youth program; he was able to avoid a prison sentence altogether; he had completed his high school equivalency; and now he was working his way up the management ladder at his current job. A proud father at age twenty-two, he felt that he needed to be a good role model to his daughter.

Far removed from the habits of his teenage years, family had become extremely important to him. His voice grew in strength as he explained, "They were a part of the reason I changed. You know, because I was a hoodlum. A gang-banger. I was a real fucking hard-ass. My mother always was there for me when I got locked up. You know, she was the one who bailed me out. And you know, my mother and sister were the ones who held me down [took care of him]. I also changed a lot being from like that because I changed for the people that was there for me. Which was my mom, my sister, my niece, my nephew, because at that time I didn't have my kids. I [recently] had my daughter. That changed me a lot. You know what I'm saying? It made me think things through."Antonio currently lived with his mother, but maintained a good relationship with his girlfriend. He prided himself on being a working man, someone who stayed focused on his duties.

This was quite a change from his former self. Before family life—before he was a responsible working man—Antonio had tasted the sweet nectar of street life. He had lived it, reaped the rewards, and to a degree he still embodied it. "You know, I was a Latin King for like eight years. You know? I'm still known in the street. I still see a couple of the old *Manitos* and shit like that. They know I work here. They don't come fuck with me. They know I did a lot of shit back in the day. So they see me here, they say *what up*, they come shopping. They don't say nothing." Antonio was in a rare position: once a high ranking member of the Latin Kings, he was able to walk away without fear of reprisal. Gang life is often difficult to walk away from as it is intended to be a lifelong commitment. He had joined a local chapter of the Kings when he was thirteen years old.

Throughout his high school years, Antonio walked the streets with a group of young thugs engaged in petty theft, public intoxication, and daily territorial disputes. Like most teenage boys from his neighborhood, he had to deal with the pressure of standing one's ground when faced with confrontation and living up to the expectations of virile masculinity.

I wondered aloud if gang activity was a mandatory coping mechanism for dealing with peer pressure. Antonio began to laugh, "I never thought that there was pressure to join gangs. I think that shit is all excuses. I never saw . . . I was a gang member for year . . ." Still standing, he leaned his weight onto a nearby railing as the memories came back to him, "I still see my peoples. I never officially got out of it. I just don't get bothered with it. If you're a gang member then you know other gang members. I've know Bloods, I've known Crips, I've known Nietas."

"Do you mean, that people look to join a gang?" I interrupted.

Clapping his hands together, "Yeah people look for it! Nobody puts a gun to your head and says *You gotta be a Blood or you gotta be a King.* You see people chillin' and throwin' up signs, and you *want* to be that! You know what I'm saying, you *want* that attention." Antonio was accustomed to the social rewards of gang life, even if it spelled greater demise in the legitimate world. Increased criminal activity tends to lead to permanent legal labels that limit traditional opportunities. Legal opportunities lead to a more laborious path for young guys like Antonio, but one does not have to worry about police officials. But in a world where he seemed to receive authoritative scrutiny, no matter how "good" he tried to be, the legitimate world was unattractive to him as a teenager. I asked him "If you could do it all over again, at the same age, would you still join a gang?"

Antonio smiled and glanced around the store, "I'm not going to lie. I think I had some of the most fun in my fucking life! You know like there were hookie parties, bitches. Yo, like orgies! I mean, gang life was crazy back in the day. We loved it. We used to go to Roosevelt High School. Roosevelt High School if you remember was on the news weekly for violence. Teachers used to get hit. We used to fuck with security guards, everything. You know what I'm saying? And that was cool."

Even though this involved daily violence, school rejection and being chased by police, for Antonio gratification was difficult to ignore. During one's teenage years, one could often not care less about how adults view them. What is more important for teenagers from any socio-economic background is the ability to climb the social totem pole.

Antonio paced back and forth in front of our interview area recalling the pleasant memories, "I used to go to Fordham Plaza, and I would start in Fordham Plaza and I'm coming with my bandana and my beads. I'd see four Latin Kings with thirty bitches. And they'd be like *Ay, yo, come over.* And then I'd look up the hill I'd see school . . ." Antonio paused as a painful look overcame his face, "I'd see security guards fucking with me, searching me, *Take your hat off! Take your belt off!* They know I'm a gang member so they want to fuck with you more. Search you harder. Tap you," he began to pat his own pockets. "You know, catch you in the halls, *What you doing in the halls? The bell rang . . .*"

Pointing to his right, Antonio continued, "Or! Here I got my mans. They got chickens. They got weed. They got beer. You know, back then forty ounces was a $1.25. You know, you got beers. You got shorties. You're about to go to a crib with music and hang out and probably get laid. You know what I'm saying? Or go to school and get fucked with by security. Have teachers bark at me, *Why you haven't been in class?* Come back after a week and they'd put you on the spot in front of everybody. You don't know what to do. You want to run back, cuss somebody out. You curse them out you get suspended . . ."

Antonio folded his arms and smirked, "So, you know what I'm saying? Go have a shitty day, or go have fun."

During this conversation, Antonio clearly laid out the choices in front of him: a) put his head down, deal with indignation, but do the right thing; or b) "go have fun." I wondered if his gender—his role as a young boy—had any bearing on his decision. In interviews that I had had with other youth, there appeared to be a distinguishable difference between the expectations of young boys and that of girls. I asked, "Do you feel that there is pressure on young boys to 'act' a certain way?"

Recognizing the sometimes exaggerated methods used to obtain the social rewards, he answered, "Yeah. Yeah. I know this guy that comes here, he spends thousands of dollars on sneakers. These people put so much pressure on each other, they'll make bets. I remember this bet for like $20,000. These two dudes were like *You bring your best twenty sneakers, and I'll bring my best twenty sneakers.* People battle each other over who has the best shit." Antonio raised his eyebrows and began to laugh, "They'll put together a panel at a sneaker convention and battle like who got the best shit. I remember there was a bet up to $50,000 at one point."

I began to fish for more information, "What about criminal behavior in general? Dealing, gang banging. . . . Do guys feel like they have to show off their money?"

"That's the pressure: Its showing off what you got. You ever see that movie *Empire*? With John Leguizamo? He's a drug dealer in the Bronx and he gets killed in the end. The first thing he says in the beginning of the movie, he says, *When it comes to the Hood, it's showing off what you got even if you don't got it.*" He snapped his fingers, "Even if you don't have a dollar in your pocket but you look like a million bucks, that's what's important. And that's what's true in all urban people's minds."

But in Antonio's eyes, times were changing. When he was younger, he believed that living by the codes of the prison subculture was a top priority. When he ran with the Latin Kings, he said his concern was less for making money and more for just having fun and maintaining his street credibility.

He was surrounded by people involved in the drug trade, but he was less interested in it because he felt it did not bring in good money. "What you see in the movies? That shit is bullshit. You don't make any money standing on the corner selling drugs. Now the guys who collect the money when these niggas re-up? They're getting money. But it takes years to get there."

Antonio was more into the street life because of the social power and the social rewards. He laughed when he thought about the crime from a decade ago compared to now, "I think before, like mid 90s. 1993 like when that gang shit started. Latin Kings came in like 1986. They didn't hit the street until like 95. So from like 1995 to 2005, that decade, was like *you got to be hood or you nothing.* I think that era was crazy to be in the hood and be a man."

To prove his worth to his peers, Antonio engaged in violent activities on a daily basis. He would often attack rival gang members or other kids in his same age group who happened to "cross his territory." It was this activity that eventually drove him into the criminal justice system. He thought ill of that behavior now, "Yeah, I mean . . . What do you really get out of beating the shit out of other people? You don't get paid for it. It's not going to give you any money. I can't go eat if I fuck you up, unless I'm robbing you."

Street life is often attractive because of the monetary rewards that can be had, but Antonio was more interested in violent capital. "I didn't rob nobody. For all the bad shit I did, I never got money out of anyone's pockets. I would fuck you up! But I would never rob you. I would beat you for fun. . . . I mean, not for fun. It was gang wars. There would be a couple of Crips or Bloods and we would be like, *Let's get these niggas here.* It was basically territorial shit. You know, Fordham Plaza was ours, *Don't cross our shit."* For all of the atrocious behaviors Antonio engaged in, at the time he believed it to be a normal part of his world.

West Bronx as Panopticon

From Antonio's perspective, official police supervision was just as much of a norm as the crime in his neighborhood. To him, this instilled a feeling of powerlessness; a way of constantly keeping his actions in check. For many young boys in the deprived dozen, the surveillance and police presence in their neighborhoods is as normal and as frequent as riding a bus across town. This reflects a larger nationwide trend of increasing police effectiveness through greater use of technology. In the West and South Bronx, there are a disproportionate amount of police officers on foot patrol (compared to the city average), inside three-wheelers (compact golf-cart like police vehicles), and an ample amount of Mobile Utility Surveillance Vehicles. A small string of homicides in the Kingsbridge neighborhood during the summer of 2007 prompted NYPD to position several of these "vans with camera towers" around the West Bronx in order to watch for potential trouble.[1]

This increased amount of eyes on the streets were intended to give the community residents a greater sense of security; all neighborhood crime would potentially have some sort of video record. But one could argue that this has the opposite effect. In Christian Parenti's *Soft Cage* (2003), he explains that this level of surveillance creates in effect an order of self-policing. "Surveillance instills discipline by forcing self-regulation."[2] With an estimated eight thousand surveillance cameras throughout New York City, many residents are used to the idea of being watched, and think nothing of it. As is said by Parenti, "The logic of such passivity is simple: if you don't have anything to hide, why be concerned?"

But of course the dynamics of police supervision change when both police officials are expecting young people to engage in criminal activity *and* young residents are tempted by mainstream values to also engage. The intimate cohabitation of poor ghettos and the criminal justice system are beginning to blur the lines between community protectionism and correctional surveillance. French sociologist Loic Wacquant (2000) would go as far to argue that "(the) ghetto and prison (are) kindred institutions of forced confinement."[3] In a city like New York—where most of its police resources are concentrated in its most deprived neighborhoods—Wacquant sees both the state prison and ghetto as serving the same function: to monitor and confine individuals without any lucrative value to society.

Penitentiaries, in their original design, were created to keep criminals "under inspection" while simultaneously looking for ways to reform them. The most important function of prisons is to allow prison officials the power of observation without giving inmates equal power. British Utilitarian Jeremy Bentham wrote about his Panopticon design through a series of letters in the late 1780s. He believed that prisons should be made for "safe custody, confinement, solitude, forced labour, and instruction."[4] Crucial to the design was its physical composition. Bentham described its architecture:

> The building is circular. The apartments of the prisoners occupy the circumference. You may call them, if you please, the *cells*. These *cells* are divided from one another, and the prisoners by that means secluded from all communication with each other, by *partitions* in the form of *radii* issuing from the circumference towards the centre, and extending as many feet as shall be thought necessary to form the largest dimension of the cell. The apartment of the inspector occupies the centre; you may call it if you please the *inspector's lodge*.[5]

This design allows for the supreme advantage of the "inspectors" while putting the inspected at the greatest disadvantage.

Michel Foucault (1977) believed that the Panopticon design was inspired by seventeenth century British efforts to quarantine towns that had been stricken by the plague. It was thought that in order to control and cease the plague, the pathological had to be contained and partitioned from the rest of society. "Those sick of the plague were caught up in a *meticulous tactical partitioning* in which individual differentiations were the constricting effects of a power that multiplied, articulated and subdivided itself."[6] Prison systems today follow this same model by incapacitating the most pathological in our society after they have been physically removed.

One could argue that New York City was "plagued" with crime during the 1970s and 1980s. The city was not considered to be a safe place, as residents avoided the subway system and dark streets even in the wealthiest of neighborhoods. Assaults, robberies and drug-related crime were commonplace. With changes in criminal justice policies—in particular with the tripling of the police force during the Giuliani-era (1993-2001)—the New York City criminal justice system moved much of this plague off of the most tourist-laden streets and went on to contain it in the most disadvantaged (and socially isolated) neighborhoods. Like towns stricken with the plague in seventeenth century England, residents in the deprived dozen find themselves engaged in a systematic process of surveillance, labeling, control and subsequent punishment.

The successful implementation of Bentham's design in actual institutions of confinement requires that it "consists in the *centrality* of the inspector's situation, combined with the well-known and most effectual contrivances for *seeing without being seen*."[7] In prisons, this is best exercised by allowing corrections officers to be centrally-seated in electronic towers where they can remotely control cell doors, or to roam freely during cell inspections while prisoners are locked inside. For pantopticon-like control of a high-crime neighborhood, this is achieved with the successful placement of police officers on foot patrol; undercover detectives roaming particular "hot spots"; strategic placement of vandal proof dome surveillance cameras; and most importantly, the very visible placement of Mobile Utility Surveillance Vehicles (MSV).

This critical mass of surveillance functions with God-like omnipresence making residents aware that they are being watched without fully being aware of the direction of the gaze. Like prisons, as Foucault would say, poor neighborhoods are under the "major effect of the Panopticon: to induce in the inmate a state of conscious and permanent visibility that assures the automatic functioning of power."[8] Residents adjust their behavior accordingly. Visitors are confronted with the possibility of crossing the lines of legality. I even caught myself doing this when walking past an MSV. Patting my pockets, I wondered, "Am I doing anything illegal? Will this small pocket knife attached to my keys get me in trouble? Did that officer just catch me jay-walking?"

Young people perceive the similarities between prisons and ghettos and view police antagonism as the "way things are" rather than something that can be eradicated. They have the choice to either comply with this power structure, or rebel against it. No other option exists. The result of the cyclical exchange between prison and ghetto creates not only the cultural and mental internalization of their identical function, but also the continued justification of reactionary police policies. As is said by Wacquant: "A ghetto is essentially a sociospatial device that enables a dominant status group in an urban setting simultaneously to *ostracize and exploit* a subordinate group endowed with *negative symbolic capital*."[9]

Take for example, the use of NYPD's *stop and frisk* program led to the normalization of police dominance over one's personal space. It is estimated that NYPD "stops" fifty-two thousand New Yorkers per year in search of illegal contraband, and most do not result in arrests.[10] For many, rather than leading to a greater sense of safety, this creates resentment and distance between officers and those whom they protect. Antonio—when asked about his experience with police contact—reiterated the normalization of being targeted by police, "I mean, there's always times . . . You know, you always get stopped for no reason. You know, you might be walking with your friend, and *you guys look suspicious*. For *probable cause*, they'll grab you and be like *Where's the gun? Where's the gun?* Or *you fit the description*, you know, for no reason."

The U.S. Supreme Court defines "probable cause" as "a reasonable belief that a person has committed a crime. [Or behavior that] warrant(s) a prudent person to believe a suspect has committed, is committing, or is about to commit a crime."[11] Therefore, the right for police to search someone on the street merely requires that the officer be "reasonable" and the individual being searched to have "potential" for criminal behavior.

Of course, putting this federal law into practice has led to many allegations of *racial profiling* and continued distrust of authority by particular neighborhood residents. In Andrew Gelman, Jeffrey Fagan, and Alex Kiss's study of NYPD's "Stop and Frisk Policy in the Context of Claims of Racial Bias" (2007), they point out that the U.S. Supreme Court allows for racial profiling "as long as there were other factors motivating the stop"[12] or "if there was an explicit racial description[13] of the suspect."[14] This has led to NYPD's informal practice of *cultural profiling:* not stopping an African American male alone, but stopping a young African American male with baggy jeans, a "du-rag," and some sort of semblance of "gang colors" in his clothing; or a young Latino male, in a hooded sweatshirt, and an "unusual bulge" in his pants pocket.

Young men like Antonio think about police contact every time they leave their homes, even if they have nothing to hide. He recounted to me, "I remember one time I was working, and I was down the block. I had just come from a bodega, me and one of my co-workers. I was smoking a cigarette right on Bainbridge. You know, the DTs [drug detectives] come and get out the car, I got my job tag on. And we're both like *We're coming from work!* And they're like *Naw. Naw.* They're patting us down like, *Where's the gun? Where's the gun? Where you came from? Why you stuttering?* And we're like, *Dude, we're coming from work. What else do you want?* And they're like, *Well, you guys fit the description. There was some murders around here.* You know, so they can't pull you over for no reason because you have to have probable cause."

"What was *their* probable cause?" I asked.

"Well, it's to search you for no reason . . ." He paused, "Well, that's their probable cause, that you *fit the description*. Or, *there was a call with two guys out robbing people with knives. . . . Somebody was out flashing a gun. . . .* You know that's their probable cause. It was you that *fit* something. *There was a robbery last night, and you guys fit the description*."

I asked how living a crime-free lifestyle affected continuous police contact, "How do you handle it now compared to before?"

"You know, I just don't care. I just let them search me and get it over with. I'm not going to fight them, because they'll lock me up for *resisting arrest*." Aware of the gray-area of legal codes officers can use to arrest youth for being provocative, Antonio knew how to navigate away from detention, "I don't have any open cases so I know I'm not going to jail. I'm not trying to be in [central] booking for two nights over some bullshit. So I don't get pissed off, like *Get the fuck off of me! I know my rights!* There's no point. When you don't say anything . . ."

He reached into his pocket, "pull out your wallet. Soon as I see them, I just pull out my wallet because I know they're going to ask for I.D. I give them my fucking I.D. That's what they're asking for, the main thing. *Give me your I.D.* They search you. You don't got anything. They give you your shit back and are like *Thank you for your cooperation.*"

Antonio raised his arms, inviting confrontation, "You start fighting, *Oh you want to be a smart-ass.* They kick you in your knee. They throw you in the car. They'll beat you on the way to the precinct just to give you a ticket. They won't even lock you up. They'll bring you all the way to the precinct. They don't want to do the paperwork, so they give you a ticket and let you go." Crossing his arms, "So to avoid all that bullshit, I give them the I.D., they search you and let you go."

For Antonio, police contact is about as frequent as waking up in the morning. The fact that he is young, Puerto Rican, lives in a high crime area, and chooses to dress in typical Hip Hop fashion only increases his chances of being searched. In the Gelman (et al) 2007 study, they concluded that "for violent and weapons offenses, blacks and Hispanics are stopped about twice as often as whites" and represented "51 percent and 33 percent of all stops while representing only 26 percent and 25 percent of the New York City population."[15] Most studies show that a disproportionate amount of stop-and-frisks occur in predominantly African American and Latino neighborhoods, with the highest rates in the South Bronx, Brownsville, and East New York.

Overbearing police presence and stop-and-frisks overall are tolerated in New York City because of the perceived benefits to the city as a whole. The 46 percent decrease in crime rates correlates well to the tripling of the size of NYPD since 1993. New Yorkers in safer neighborhoods feel more at ease as "all of the criminals are sent upstate." Even Antonio believed he reaped some of the benefits when I asked him if "his neighborhood was safe."

"Compared to what it was like before? And a lot of neighborhoods that are in the borough? I think my neighborhood is pretty pretty safe. There's a lot more police. Like when I lived on 170 . . ." He paused to think, "Once you go to the Concourse, you see much more cops on the Concourse [Boulevard]. Two cops on Walton [Street]. Three on Wyck [Street]. You know what I'm saying, it's much more heavily 'thinged' then before. I remember going up there, and there was constant gun shots. All the time on 171 and Morris. You know, because I'm right in front of Taft High School, so you know, that area was known for violence. You know, you got Sheridan [Avenue]. Which is a hot block. 172 and Sheridan. Tilden [Avenue]. And then Morris, which has always been hot, too. So I used to constantly hear gunfire. People always getting killed. In the park behind me, Claremont [Park], there was always murders and rapes. So compared to the way it was when I was younger to now I think it's *real* good."

I pulled for more, "What do you think changed?

"I think, to me, most of the people who was doing all the violent shit is in jail. I heard a lot of those people are locked up. I think it's more . . . more of just the *presence* of the cops. They are constantly running. . . . Even though it's not hot now, you still see guys constantly rolling around, you know what I'm saying the DTs, the black [Chevy] Impalas. You can always tell who are the detectives. They're not really *that* undercover. I think they do that on purpose, so they like *We're here. Don't fuck around*."

Also contributing to police culture in New York is the increase of "Special Units." Whether traffic, school safety, or narcotics detectives, NYPD now has over three hundred specialized units, each dedicated to particular crimes. To Antonio, this has worked to his advantage, "Blue and whites [for more general code enforcement] will lock you up for anything. They don't give a fuck what it is. You got an empty bag of weed, they'll lock you up for that. DTs? Actual detectives, not blue and whites, they don't lock you up for anything." He recounted a time when he thought he was going to be arrested, "I got pulled over by a DT and I had a long-ass knife. They didn't even get out the car. They was like, *Come over here. What are you doing around here?* Then they was like *You got something on you?* I was like *yeah.* Gave my I.D. with the knife."

Antonio leaned towards me and smirked, "The nigga gave me my I.D. *and* the knife back. I've seen them pull over my brother. He had weed in the gas compartment. They searched the whole car. One nigga saw this little piece of plastic. They pulled it out, it was a half ounce of weed. They gave it back to him and was like *Get the fuck outta here.* And they was like *We're looking for snow.* Which is cocaine. And they was like *If there's not cocaine or drugs, then we don't give a fuck.* So it just depends on what category of police you're talking about."

A Path for Redemption

After a long fun-filled taste of street life, Antonio understood it was time to move on as he started to trek through his adult years. With the various amount of tools he had under his belt, he knew that he could have had a different life, "I think now if I could do it all over again I would have went back to school, finished school when I was supposed to, went to college." Looking around the store, he contemplated, "Right now I would have been graduating from college. I would have got my diploma in 2004 because I went to high school in 2000. So now I would have been graduating from college. So if I went back with the mentality that I have now, I would have been like *fuck these niggas* [his former friends]. *Let me go to school so I can get that good job*. I'll have all that fun. I'll have money to pay for my own cell and go clubbing. You know, I wasn't thinking like that back then. At that age I was fourteen, I wasn't trying to go to school, *I'm trying to party. I'm trying to go clubbing.* I'd be home at three in the afternoon with a hangover. Like *Oh shit, that was a long day.* Like it was at night or something."

He began to smile again, "It was fun, I'm not going to fucking lie. I had some crazy fun. You know, going to the parade, the Puerto Rican parade, you would walk and people would like looking at you like, *Oh!* You know, you would get their attention. It was all about the attention. But now, it's nothing." Pointing to the store, "Now I'm here selling sneakers."

To Antonio the magnetism of street life is not a difficult sentiment to feel. It made for warm memories and wild stories, but only after removal from his adolescent years could he fully understand the consequences of his actions. I asked if he could imagine himself being involved in these activities at that moment.

Shaking his head from side to side he responded, "No! I don't want to go to jail. I went to Rikers and that shit was horrible. And I was like, *I can't understand why people are proud of this.* You know you got people coming back saying, *You know I did five years. I did six months.* You know and I'm like, *What the fuck are you proud of? What's so cool?* You know, you can't do nothing in there. If you got a personal habit, you know . . . You know, like, I can't get high in there. I can't get drunk. I can't go clubbing. I see no women. What's so cool that there's nothing to be proud of? If you come out of jail, that don't make you bullet proof. You come out of jail, I shoot you in the head and then you done. You know? There's nothing that makes you any better from coming out of jail than a blot on your record." A more serious look dominated his face, "My mother might catch a heart attack if I go to jail again. Because she took it very bad the first time. She even fainted and that. So I was like, *There's no point in this."*

Antonio now had more concern for his family: his mother, his daughter, and the influence of his behavior on his younger male relatives, "If I could change it, I would 100 percent go back. Fuck it. I would have been the nerd. *Fuck it if everyone picks on me*. I would have been right up there after college in an intern in a firm or something. . . ." Rubbing his chin, "I *do* like the fact that I know people. I mean, I got family members and they are just dumb to the streets. I mean, they so don't know anything. My nephew is like sixteen. He got problems in school. He gets bullied all the time. He gets bullied by *girls*. That nigga is taller than me! He's like this (holding his hand above his head). Sixteen years old, getting bitched by girls. I be getting calls like, *I don't know what to do, Antonio.* You know, that is the one thing that I'm happy that I have; that I know the street."

Antonio was conflicted over the value of his new found mentality over street life, and price of his past experience, "If I see a group of niggas, I know if someone is coming at me or not. You know, I won't be scared because I already know what to watch out for. I know if someone is talking about me sideways. I already know if they're talking about me or the next nigga. I got that street smarts. I'm not scared to fight nobody." Sighing as if to control his emotions, he continued, "I'm not saying it's good to be violent, but I'm not going to be a pussy. I'm not going to have some girls snatch me up in school. I mean, how you going to get fucked by girls? You got people smacking you up in school. And that's something I'm happy I didn't go through. I mean, being the punk also fucks up your school."

There is a fine line a young man has to walk if he wants to keep his head down in order to not be involved in street life while at the same time not being scathed by it, "I knew this kid; a straight A student. They didn't want to transfer him out. He got jumped. They caught him with a knife, now they want to transfer him out the school. Now he got to stay in school getting messed with; getting bullied. And for nothing; because he's a good kid. He didn't do anything worth shit, he was just scared. Being too nice, now he doesn't want to be good anymore. Now he feels like he's got to be a man."

As Antonio recounted the tough struggle to maintain a "good boy's" identity in a world that allow for it, I began to wonder how a young boy raised in the deprived dozen could avoid street life. Antonio was part of a lucky few who walked both paths at the crossroad and was still able to walk away with a fresh life in front of him. A felony conviction will not be limiting his job opportunities in the future, something afforded to him because of his participation in an ATI program. He can abstain from a criminal lifestyle because of the support network around him. Yet, he will also be able to use his street smarts to avoid being a victim of crime, something he can use to protect his family. This all comes from the knowledge he obtained from both worlds, a set of tools that many social programs are trying harness for all crime-engaged youth.

Notes

1. Appel, H. (2007, July 12). "Assaults, Murder on Kingsbridge Bring Increased Surveillance." Retrieved from Norwood News website on July 18, 2010: http://www.norwoodnews.org/story/?id=89&story=assaults,+murder+on+kingsbridge+bring+increased+surveillance.

2. Parenti, Christian. *The Soft Cage: Surveillance in America.* New York, N.Y.: Basic Book, 2003.

3. Wacquant, Loic (2000). "The New Peculiar Institution: On the Prison as Surrogate Ghetto." *Theoretical Criminology.* Vol. 4(3). 377-389.

4. Bentham, Jeremy. *The Panopticon Writings.* Ed. Miran Bozovic. London, United Kingdom: Verso, 1995.

5. Bentham, p. 35.

6. Foucault, Michel. *Discipline and Punish: The Birth of the Prison.* New York, N.Y.: Vintage Books, 1977.

7. Bentham, p. 43.

8. Foucault, p. 201.

9. Wacquant, p. 383.

10. Rivera, R., Baker, A., and Roberts, J. (2010, July 11). "A few blocks, 4 years, and 52,000 police stops." *The New York Times, p. A1.*

11. U.S. v. Puerta, 982 F.2d 1297, 1300 (1992).

12. Whren et al v. U.S. (1996).

13. Brown v. Oneonta (2000)

14. Gelman, A., Fagan, J. and Kiss., A. (2007). "An Analysis of the New York City's Police Department's 'Stop and Frisk' Policy in the Context of Claims of Racial Bias." *Journal of the American Statistical Association,* Vol. 102, No. 479, p. 813-823.

15. Gelman et al, p. 821.

Chapter 7: Pedagogy of the Deprived: Program Support for Structural Deficiencies

"Yeah, we run things in there!" A smirk grew on the left side of Malik's face. "We run things in Rikers. The C.O.s got *no* power in there!" Slouching deeper into his chair, Malik shimmied his baseball cap a couple of millimeters below his eyebrows—as if to shield himself from the anticipated responses.

"*God*, Malik. Why are you so stupid sometimes?" Jasmin turned and faced a nearby friend while shaking her head.

Flanked by two teenage girls in the middle of the table, Malik patiently waited as other members of the group began to respond. The girls dominated the airspace with teeth-sucking and exaggerated exhales.

The boys smiled and laughed to themselves.

Tall and husky, Assadullah stood at the head of the table with a perplexed gaze, "How can you run things when you don't even have control over your own privacy? That sounds a lot like what *House Niggers* used to think." His voice rose, "The House Nigger may be treated well, have some privileges, and eventually think that he is in control of the house; but in truth he is, and *always* will be, just like the *Field Nigger:* a slave."

Malik's smirk disappeared as he turned his head to the side. Like many of the participants of the Each One Teach One Youth Leadership Training Program, he was navigating through the popularized magnetism of the hustler class and the normalization of prison as a rite of passage into manhood.

"I'm no *House* Nigga!" Malik sat up in his chair, "I'm talking about the little things we do on the side." He clasped his hands together and flipped them over, "You know? A little smoke here, snacks there. We play whatever we want and watch what we want on the TV. The C.O.s can't say nothin!"

A couple of the boys nodded their heads in agreement.

Malik has preached the gospel of a proud tradition of incarceration—something that many of his cousins experienced before him—*passage into manhood by fire*. There is an acceptance of confinement as a mechanism for strengthening one's character, especially if one can eke out a small piece of personal empowerment from an institution that is designed to concede none.

As many of the girls continued to sigh, Assadullah shook off Malik's bravado, "Don't you understand that being in jail, or being out there on the street selling drugs, or being in a gang only contribute to social problems?" He paused with some intensity, petting his beard, "You're doing *exactly* what they want you to do." Like most nights at the Each One Teach One program, Assadullah found an opportunity to challenge the conventional thinking of New York teens. His intentions were to encourage critical thinking while avoiding humiliation.

The kids of Each One Teach One hailed from all over the city, most of them from the deprived dozen. Places such as Harlem, South Jamaica, and Bedford-Stuyvesant are highly segregated neighborhoods, with high rates of crime, small amounts of wealth, and sub-standard public education. These teens were all enrolled in high school, but only a handful were expected to graduate. Legally they were children, but they had to grow up fast. They acquired street smarts that may never lead to legitimate opportunities but that afforded them survival in a trying environment.

Housed in a small Victorian Era brownstone in the Greenwich Village neighborhood of Manhattan, the Each One Teach One (EOTO) program recruited teenagers from local high schools in an effort to mold their street smarts into practical, real-world intelligence. Founded in 1997 by the Correctional Association of New York, the program focused on building "the organizational and leadership skills of young people who have been affected by juvenile justice policies."[1] Even though it was not a traditional ATI program, the Each One Teach One Youth Leadership Training program gathered volunteers that were often court-involved. It was a community-oriented, grass-roots organization that acted as a counterweight to the sometimes deficient public educational institutions of New York's poorest neighborhoods.

Typically running twice a year in four-month cycles, I joined EOTO in January 2006 as a volunteer, mentor, and ethnographer. This particular group consisted of six boys and eight girls. All of them exuded the charisma, defensiveness, and tactical wit typical of teenagers raised in New York City. They all faced the hedonistic enticements of teenage life. Some chose to look past them and focus on their future, while others—particularly the boys—lived in the moment, willingly indulging in these enticements as a means to savor the sweet taste of neighborhood admiration.

Confined by the finite choices of neighborhood deprivation, many of these teens saw their opportunities as limited; some only envisioned a singular path. As was said in Paulo Friere's *Pedagogy of the Oppressed* (1970), "the oppressed, instead of striving for liberation, tend themselves to become oppressors, or 'sub-oppressors.' The very structure of their thought has been conditioned by the contradictions of the concrete, existential situation by which they were shaped."[2] Many do not look to free themselves from structural deprivation, nor see the point in striving to do so.

Seventeen-year-old Malik volunteered to participate in the program's activities but was conflicted about his desire to maintain a delinquent public persona. After already serving two years in Brookwood Correctional Facility for stolen property, drug charges—and what he claimed was an attempted murder charge—he was acquainted with the informal decree required to gain *street respect*. But he was also aware that street respect could also shorten his life.

In a separate one-on-one interview, he stated that "(young) men are pressured into selling drugs, doing robberies, hanging on the corner . . . doing dumb stuff." He claimed that selling narcotics was a "bad route (and that) fast money is dead money." Although he had a keen awareness of the end game of street life, these sentiments never seemed to surface during the group format of the training program. The division between these two philosophies was a common theme among all of the teen.

Each One Teach One and the Cultural Empowerment Model

The Each One Teach One Youth Leadership Training Program was the services and advocacy arm of the Juvenile Justice Project at the Correctional Association of New York. This program utilized alternative educational tools and had three main goals at its core:

1) To train young people to become activists and leaders in juvenile justice reform efforts.
2) To involve young people in the public debate and decision-making regarding youth and juvenile justice issues.
3) To effect positive, far-reaching changes in juvenile justice policies in New York.[3]

The training program aimed not only to educate youth to their legal rights but also to change the mindset that places them on the path to state confinement, a method I refer to as the Cultural Empowerment Model.

One of the goals of the program was to provide youth with an alternative response to the conditions that they deal with on a daily basis; particularly in contrast to the services they receive in their local high schools. The United States public education system has a reputation for producing the "C students" of the world in math and reading. This underachievement is most acute in New York City's public schools as well as in major urban areas of the "rust belt" in general.

According to the Citizens' Committee for Children of New York, Inc., New York City as a whole has a 7.6 percent dropout rate. But dropout rates increase to 14.6 percent when looking at the Bronx alone and 12.1 percent when looking at Brooklyn.[4] African American and Latino students have the lowest chances of completing high school, with Latinos having the highest dropout rates at 17.6 percent. In New York's poorest neighborhoods, more than 60 percent of students are not meeting the state's and city's reading and math requirements. Although these issues have been brought to light by many researchers, New York's schools continue to have problems with overcrowding, outdated library books, and a reluctance to incorporate more twenty-first century technology.

Even more disparaging is the difference in school performance between boys and girls. High school age boys are 25 percent more likely to drop out of school, as only 63.5 percent are meeting graduation requirements compared to the 73.8 percent of girls who meet requirements.[5] Evidence of the gender gap between boys and girls persists not only on the street, but also inside school walls.

Low performance rates have been viewed at times as a cultural or class issue with little responsibility put on the educational institutions themselves. Historically, the worst schools (in terms of underperformance) have typically been in poor and/or minority communities. Since the 1950s, there has been discussion as to whether community members are the causal force behind the poor performance or whether it is related to structural forces.

In the political climate immediately following the *Brown vs. the Board of Education* decision of 1954, many began to postulate that "if the differences in school achievement were not genetic then they had to be the result of some other deficit, *or,* caused by persistent unequal treatment, that is, individual and institutional bias. Preponderance of social policy and social science thinking chose the former, which opened the door for the rise to prominence of "cultural deficit" arguments."[6]

From this thinking emerged the concept of "cultural deprivation" in the 1960s, which was a partial throwback to Social Darwinist claims of "behavioral determinism" as a certainty for particular cultural (or ethnic) groups. In G. Honor Fagan's *Culture, Politics and Irish School Dropouts* (1995), he outlined the basic premise and implications of this theory:

> Within a cultural deprivation theory of poverty, poor people are seen to be a part of the larger culture but, yet, not sufficiently socialized into that culture . . . They are deprived of the part of the culture that enables success. The deprived culture is passed on in a cyclical fashion through the socialization of children, which includes particular "inadequate" child-rearing practices.[7]

According to this perspective, the education system cannot be held responsible for the underperformance of poor and minority youth.

Popular in the 1960s was Oscar Lewis' *Culture of Poverty Theory.*[8] At the time, social sciences tended to treat deprivation (and anomie) as a choice. The cultural values and norms of poor and working-class families stood in vivid contrast to the norms and values of mainstream middle-class America. It was believed that these differences were centered on the "peculiar" teachings of poor families. Like many other occasions in the social sciences, there was a failure to recognize social structure in these collective deficiencies.

Historically, New York City has been a leader in the services industry for children. In the early 1800s, it had one of the first public institutions dedicated to primary education. The purpose of this distributive structure was to prepare citizens for a cooperative adjustment to the emerging world. Throughout the 19th century in particular, public education served as a means of preparing young men for industrial work. As was professed by a member of the Rockefeller Education Board (a large monetary contributor to education) in 1906, "The task we set before ourselves is simple, we will organize children and teach them to do in a perfect way the things their fathers and mothers are doing in an imperfect way." One could even argue that this system was preparing an entire society for industrial perfection, i.e., by teaching young people how to do "menial tasks repeatedly, remain docile and respond to Pavlovian bells."[9]

One hundred and fifty years later, the pedagogical mechanics of public education in poor urban communities have remained unchanged. Still centered on a model that produces industrial workers, it is *under*-preparing young people for post-industrial work. Across class lines, every culture recognizes the necessity of a post-secondary education for legitimate success in today's society. Universities are our current retainers of what Michel Foucault (1970) would call the necessary "code of knowledge"[10] for perseverance in the twenty-first century. If social mobility requires—in most cases—a quality college education, then this must be preceded by quality primary and secondary education. Even Bill Gates claims that class mobility is impossible without a college degree, but clearing the path to the university should be the primary concern.

Public education was designed to provide a means of competition for all people. As stated by Jonathan Kozol in *Savage Inequalities* (1991), "denial of the means of competition is perhaps the single most consistent outcome of the education offered to poor children in the schools of our largest cities."[11] Until the education system is updated to teach realistic sustainability in the post-industrial job market, high unemployment and crime rates will inevitably occur. To bring urban American teens into the post-industrial world, a new opportunity structure is necessary.[12] Public education is particularly important because it is designed to provide concrete opportunities and access to lucrative employment. When these opportunities are lacking in our largest structures, sometimes smaller, more grass-roots organizations step in to do the work.

In Each One Teach One's quest to build a micro-opportunity structure for their participants, they were keenly aware that cultural as well as structural issues needed to be addressed. Liberating them from the confines of educational deprivation required an alternative approach to thinking about these conditions; and it required that the participants were able to relate to the instructors. As was said by Paolo Friere, "This lesson and this apprenticeship must come, however, from the oppressed themselves and from those who are truly solidary [*sic*] with them." To undo the overwhelming expectations of failure, the teens of EOTO needed to hear it from someone who had disentangled himself from the stereotypical notions of being poor and uneducated.

As a mentor, role model and facilitator, Assadullah recognized that his purpose was to enlighten youth and to guide them toward new decisions. The core function of the group sessions was to inform and redirect the participants' thoughts toward positive alternative choices . . . even to media and neighborhood influences. His was a very "active education,"[13] as was propagated by historic educational reformer John Dewey, which included group activities, problem solving, as well as movie discussions.

On one particular Thursday evening, Assadullah began the group by talking about army recruitment. While circling the table, he handed out a photocopied cartoon depicting a young man having trouble maintaining employment. The second frame of the cartoon featured the young man being laid off "one time too many." In the third, he had decided to join the army with the promise of a better future. By the fourth frame, he had discovered that the army was not what it had promised, so he wanted to quit. An army recruiter laughed and said, "You signed a contract, now I have your *stankin' ass* forever!"

After everyone read the cartoon, Assadullah asked, "So who here has ever thought about joining the army?" Three hands fired into the air. Felix interjected, "I wanted to join after I saw the film *Jarhead*. It seemed like a place where guys could cool-out. Lots of camaraderie. A place to build a family . . . "

"Then you kill someone!" Simone chose to help Felix finish his sentence.

"I think my desire faded after a couple of days . . ."

"Then you kill someone!"

Tanisha jumped in with her impassioned view on the war in Iraq, "That war ain't nothing about us. Bush said this war was about 9/11, but Saddam ain't connected to Al Qaeda. It's not your war!"

The room was split on the pros and cons of a military career. Danielle stated that her aspirations for the military were based on the college benefits and work skills that are promised in the advertisements. Tanisha, Jasmin, John, and Jessica were most adamantly against military recruitment, while Felix and Angela spoke in its defense. Angela had done her own research on training and safety, stating, "You can opt out of service after basic training, and you could also opt out of combat once you join."

Leaning over the table, supporting his weight on the edge, Assadullah steered the conversation into a comparison between the military and prison structure: "One is not free in either institution." Like social-psychologist Erving Goffman's (1961) conceptualization of the *total institution,* Assadullah saw the prison and the military as places where the participant is "broken down and built back up" for the benefit of order. Although he was very subjective in his view of the military, Assadullah wanted to provide an alternative perspective on an institution that is typically sold as the only stable option for underprivileged teens in a bad economy.

His comments provided a easy transition to two short documentary films: *The Stanford University Prison Experiment* (1971) and *The Attica Uprising* (1971). Each film had its own take on the function of prisons. The Stanford film depicted how power can easily lead to cruelty and inhumane treatment, while the Attica film showed how inhumane treatment inevitably leads to struggle and resistance.

Shortly afterward, Assadullah began a discussion on the difference between a "riot" and an "uprising." The participants' eyes beamed with attention as they learned that prisoners held Attica's staff hostage and forced the New York governor to negotiate terms to improve their conditions.

"I can't believe they took over the whole prison!" Malik exclaimed.

"They were stupid to think the governor was to going to let them free," Tanisha interjected.

The participants were already familiar with the distinction between an uprising and a riot, as Assadullah had explained this dichotomy in past sessions. He reiterated, "Remember, an uprising has a purpose, while a riot is aggression without *any* purpose."

"You mean like the L.A. riots?" Felix wondered.

"Exactly, where brothers were breaking up their own businesses."

With a short pause and a glance around the room, Assadullah asked to open air, "So, are you a riot, or an uprising?" Without hesitation, all twelve participants simultaneously exclaimed, "An uprising!!" Jasmin quietly leaned toward Simone and whispered, "But I can be a riot sometimes. When someone starts pushing my buttons . . ."

As is the case with any successful system of education, Assadullah began each session by requiring the participants to engage in critical thought. Then he provided the group with a select few case studies and a requirement to study them. Although idiosyncratic—and sometimes biased in his views—he provided a set of unconventional tools for his participants to use in conventional situations. Whether dealing with police contact, searching for extra tutoring for school work, or making them aware of the function of some of the larger institutions (such as the military), Assadullah was always intent on pushing their minds beyond acceptance of low standards of living, or, worse, of chronic incarceration.

Assadullah's innovative style began by making them think about themselves. On one occasion, he set up the group in a circle for a discussion and simply asked, "What is your prison?" He wanted the participants to think about this question metaphorically and to consider what they "could not live without." The intended lesson was that vice, addiction, habit, and even cultural expectation could imprison individuals in an unchanging mode of behavior. Many of the participants began to talk about brand name clothing and jewelry as their vice. By the end of the discussion, Assadullah had steered the conversation toward the expectations of being "street" or "thug," reiterating that "just because you have a certain pigmentation to your skin does not mean that a predetermined set of behaviors comes with it." His purpose was to deconstruct cultural norms as a means to create personal empowerment.

The kids of Each One Teach One had considerable anxiety regarding how to navigate their environments. Peer pressure, on the one hand, and institutional pressure, on the other, were pulling them in different directions. Assadullah's leadership training course provided them with a safe space to discuss their angst and to discover unforeseen alternate pathways.

I conducted one-on-one interviews with several of the participants to determine whether they changed how they maneuver their environments. As stated by

Angela, "[the program taught] me how to build confidence. How to make new friends. It gave me the ability to share my opinion. It helped me to know that I have rights." As a part of the program, the participants learned detailed insider knowledge of the correctional system. Because police contact had become the norm, this was the most attractive aspect of the program to most of the youth.

Each youth may have reacted differently to the information provided, but each came away with something. Some attended for more practical reasons, such as Daniel, who claimed that "I come here to stay out of trouble." Others attended to learn a new set of skills, such as Felix, who claimed, "I learned more about the criminal justice system. How to empower youth. I learned how to make change in a positive way."

The importance of deconstructing racial stereotypes, the reward for moving above and beyond the deprived expectations of today's adolescents, and the intentions of the program as a whole surfaced when I spoke to each participant. Each of them offered kind words when I asked them what they learned from the program. "I learned how to be a better leader," proclaimed Malik.

"It kept me out of trouble . . . It keeps me from robbing people!" LeSean laughed.

"Reality. They don't teach us this stuff in school," explained Susie. "You know, I don't get in trouble with the law. I'm not interested in that stuff. I'm here to get more information." Like most of the kids of Each One Teach One, Sally seemed satisfied with the product. "I'm willing to open my mind more. I can see more outside the box."

Like many ATI programs throughout New York City, EOTO was designed to fill the voids created by institutional neglect. Adolescents have several categories of issues to deal with, so much so that it would be difficult for New York City's municipal structure to keep up with. Whether it's poor education, coping with police practices unfriendly to teenagers, or dealing with slim mental health services, one just has to look between the cracks to find program initiatives that treat these issues.

Brooklyn TASC and the Mental Health Institutional Nexus Model

Continued incarceration of adolescents in New York City is in part due to the human services that do not reach them. Although we may look at public education as a major culprit—because of its availability to all—it cannot take all of the blame. When looking at the conditions that often lead youth into the criminal justice system—whether its poor education, police presence, familial deficiencies, or differential exposure—what is often left out of the conversation is the lack of institutional support for mental health hygiene.

A large percentage of adolescents who pass through the criminal justice system are dealing with heightened mental health or substance abuse problems, but the court system tends to punish the crime rather than consider the myriad of impulses driving young criminal offenders. As a result, most juvenile offenders with mental health issues are filtered through the criminal justice system like anyone else. The New York State Division of Criminal Justice of Justice Services estimates that "between 50 to 70 percent of incarcerated youth have a diagnosable mental illness."[14] Fox Butterfield of the *New York Times* estimated that 16 percent of the jail population throughout the nation has a diagnosed mental illness.[15]

Although the majority of ATI programs in New York City deal with the legal and cultural issues affecting crime-engaged youth, a handful deal specifically with what many consider to be a "mental health crisis." Brooklyn Adolescent Link (BAL) was founded in 2000 under the New York City Treatment Alternatives for Safer Communities (TASC) program with the intention of linking "seriously emotionally disturbed adolescents returning to the Brooklyn community from the NYC Juvenile/Criminal Justice into services to insure that they achieve their optimum level of function and avoid hospitalization and/or reincarceration."[16] This program provided much needed attention to the mental health problems of adolescent offenders by creating a network for inpatient and outpatient mental health treatment; a system of referrals that I call the Mental Health Institutional Nexus Model.

Most of the adolescents coming into the criminal justice system are also from communities with high rates of "serious emotional disturbance" (SED). (See figure 7a.) SED is a general category for any diagnosable mental, behavioral or emotional disorders affecting children. Jeff Buck and Tami Mark (2006) estimate that 9 to 13 percent of all children in the United States have some sort of SED.[17] Where a small number of youth in New York City (8,895) are receiving licensed mental health services, many others end up incarcerated for behavioral problems.

Drug use amongst juveniles is widespread throughout the United States. This is a likely contributor to deviant and/or criminal behavior. According to the U.S. Department of Justice's *Juvenile Offenders and Victims: National Report* (2006), among high school age youth 76.6 percent use alcohol, 46 percent use marijuana, 14 percent use amphetamines and 13 percent use some sort of narcotic: all contributing to the already impaired judgment of adolescents.[18] With this in mind, Brooklyn Adolescent Link targeted a population whom they considered to have "enhanced impairments." They addressed a variety of mental health issues, including cases of substance abuse, Attention Deficit Hyperactive Disorder, Adjustment Disorder, Conduct Disorder and Post-Traumatic Stress Disorder (resulting from some sort of physical or sexual abuse).

Outside of case management, court advocacy, and personal counseling, most of Brooklyn Adolescent Link's services were not "in-house." Unlike BronxConnect or Andrew Glover, there were no on-site group activities or life skills sessions. Their survival kit consisted of a referral system to outpatient (community) and inpatient (residential) treatment centers throughout New York City that deal specifically with SED disorders. This network provided BAL with

Figure 7a: SED Compared to Juvenile Arrests in New York City

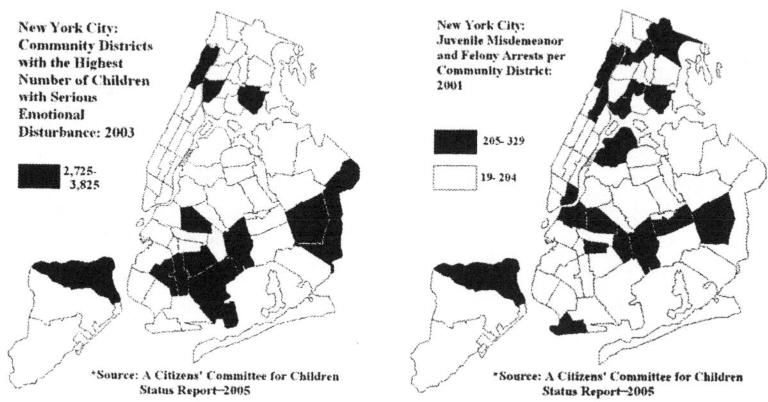

a variety of choices depending on the needs of the client. Because the BAL program acted as an axis point between several agencies, they did most of their work inside of the court room.

I connected with Brooklyn Adolescent Link beginning in 2006 strictly as an observer and interviewer. On one spring morning, I sat with the BAL Program Director in Brooklyn Criminal Court to observe their court advocacy efforts.

The featured case was being held in the screening and treatment enhancement part. BAL's court report centered on a young man named Chris, who had been in Brooklyn Adolescent Link for close to two years and was receiving substance abuse counseling. The case manager presented the court report to the court officer, who then handed it to the judge. The judge leaned back in his chair and adjusted his glasses as he browsed over the report. He then spoke to the case manager, "Do you have anything to add to what is written?"

"Only that Chris is in good standing and we recommend an early discharge from the program," the case manager quickly responded.

The judge removed his glasses and spoke directly to Chris from the bench, "This is outstanding! This is the triple-crown: perfect attendance, a negative toxicology *and* you're working. Very few are able to achieve the triple-crown." The judge motioned to release Chris from community supervision and to grant him "Youthful Offender" status. He did so with a smile as he stood and extended his arm across the bench for a handshake. Chris made his way to the bench and shook his hand as the judge beckoned for the court's involvement, "Let's give this guy a round of applause!" Chris's family, court advocates and people who did not even know him stood to clap.

Some of BAL's clients were not so successful. Some had failed drug tests, or failed to comply with outpatient treatment regiments. One client in particular was scheduled to attend an outpatient program for substance abuse, but he was arrested for a new charge between court dates, so the judge ordered that he be placed in Daytop Residential Treatment Facility. Like other ATI programs, failure to comply with court mandates typically leads to placement in a residential treatment facility or in detention.

Rare in the ATI world are programs like Brooklyn Adolescent Link, which deal with populations who may have an impediment to rational thought. They were there to convince the Criminal Court system to consider past criminal record, mental deficiencies, adolescent thinking, and substance abuse; essentially, anything that can impair a person's free thinking. BAL's specialty was in providing the court a "pre-plea investigation," which also included a psychological evaluation. Judges had to study the result of this investigation to determine which course of action was best for the individual *and* the community. In the case of Brooklyn Adolescent Link, they handled the cases permitted by the courts to treat mental health and substance abuse issues. Most of these clients came from the same neighborhoods as the adolescent offenders that are failing to adjust to poor structural conditions. Subsequently, there may be a link between these deprived neighborhoods and the high rates of diagnosable mental illness among the adolescent offender population.

In Response to "Ghetto Fatigue"

The term "ghetto fatigue" (ghetto *schwachkeit*) was first used to describe the "crowding, shortage of basic necessities, harsh environmental and sanitary conditions . . . chronic under-nutrition, physical and mental exhaustion" of Jews in Holocaust conditions of World War II Germany.[19] Although not as severe, in the context of New York City this could be used to describe the shortage of basic necessities and the resultant mental exhaustion of those living in New York's deprived dozen. The borough of Brooklyn in particular has some of the highest concentrations of poverty, the most hyper-segregated schools (above 80 percent of one race), and four of the top ten neighborhoods with the highest rates of children with serious emotional disturbance.[20]

When a combination of several detrimental conditions are heaped on top of each other—including racial segregation, poverty, a dilapidated job market, poor education, and deteriorating family structure—the result can only be continued mental distress and a downward spiral into anomic behavioral practices. This has been recognized for decades, yet little has changed. As was said by William J. Wilson and Loic Wacquant (1988) in their discussion of the 1968 Kerner Report on poverty:

> The report concluded that among the leading causes of racial strife visited upon urban America during the previous four summers were the continued exclusion of great numbers of blacks from the benefits of economic progress, the concentration of poor blacks in major cities, and the restriction of black ghettos, where segregation and poverty converged to *destroy opportunity and enforce failure*.[21] [my emphasis]

In that same year, President Lyndon B. Johnson declared a "war on poverty," where he was intent on dismantling the conditions that lead to poverty and crime. At the time there were thirty-four million Americans living below the poverty line. Today, there are thirty-five million living below the poverty line, showcasing little change.

Another factor contributing to the mental health of Brooklyn's youth is the high rate of violent crimes in the poorest neighborhoods (an indication of the anomic behavioral patterns resulting from structural deprivation). Since the 1960s, Brooklyn has continued to have the highest rates of violent crimes in New York City, most notably with little change in particular neighborhoods. (See figure 7b.) New York City has seen a 46 percent decrease in crime since 1993,[22] but the areas with the highest concentration of crime still remain the same.[23] New York State focuses most of its crime prevention budget in the incarceration of individuals from these neighborhoods, while doing very little to reduce the conditions that cause crime.

Adolescents responding to the forces of structural deprivation, and the expectation of inevitable imprisonment, are likely to develop a social-psychosis that is conducive to deviant behavior. The three most common disorders encountered by Brooklyn Adolescent Link—Adjustment Disorder (characterized by anxiety, depression and behavioral issues), Conduct Disorder (a precursor to anti-social personality disorder), and Attention Deficit Hyperactive Disorder—can be said to have social causes. Sigmund Freud's career in psychoanalysis was based on the idea that most "crime is an expression of buried internal conflicts that result from traumas and deprivations during childhood."[24] If a neighborhood continues to reproduce a crime-causing environment, then teenagers raised in these neighborhoods are likely to incorporate criminal activity into their psyches.

The task of Brooklyn Adolescent Link was to act as a pioneering force in addressing these mental health issues. In an interview with two of their forensic case managers, they explained that their occupation is "so much more than just case management. We act as therapists, mentors and court advocates." Their job was to act as the pivot in the wheel of social, familial, psychological and judicial services. They were aware of the cultural *and* structural influences that drive young people to criminal behavior. One of the case managers explained, "These kids are growing up in an environment where crime is the only option. They are ignorant of the basics of human rights."

One of BAL's clients, Justin, believed that he was lucky to have received services in the Link program. Diagnosed by one of the out-patient providers with schizophrenia, Justin had been homeless at a young age after dealing with unavoidably destitute conditions, "My mom was sick with a heart problem, cancer *and* a mental illness. I was sent to a group home at the age of fifteen. But I ran back home. My mom and I were eventually evicted; then I caught a case." As I sat with Justin, he appeared emotionally distressed even though he was far

Figure 7b: Reported Assaults and Murders in New York City—2010

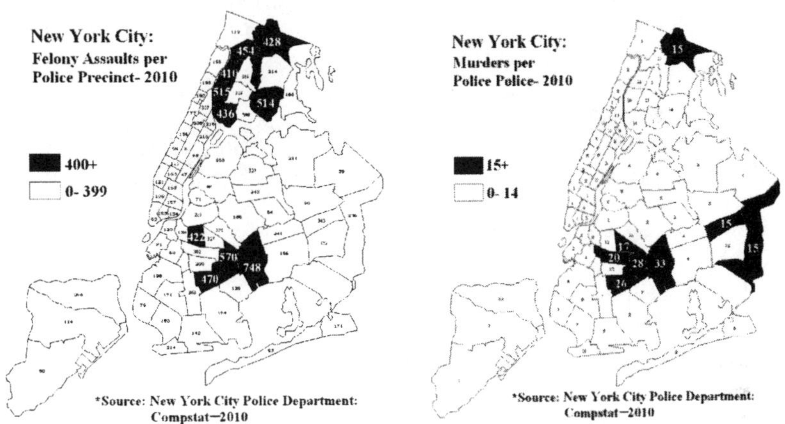

removed from this period in his life. "I spent time in jail. Then I was released and lived in a shelter. But I went back to jail. When I got out, I ended up having to rob people." Justin looked at me and smiled. "Well . . . I didn't *have to* but . . . Sometimes I would panhandle. Then I got knocked for the robbery. I was on the train. I had to cut someone who tried to take my jacket."

Justin was so used to the hardened life of surviving on his own in East Flatbush, Brooklyn that he was able to speak about his history with a very matter-of-fact tone. He considered himself to be a changed man, someone who "used to have issues with socializing with people. My hygiene wasn't that good. My mental wasn't up there. Now I know how to handle those things." As we sat and talked, I noticed his freshly pressed Adidas jumpsuit and impeccably clean sneakers.

Even though Justin recognized that he had a "choice" when it came to robbing people on the New York City subway, he represented one of many youth who see it as a "practical" choice. Had he not been discovered by the BAL program, he probably would have continued to engage in crime in order to survive. I had asked what his situation would be like without the program. He explained, "It would be different. I would probably be running the streets. The program inspired me to grow and become a man. I would have had a chip on my shoulder if I served big time in prison." Intensely gazing the floor between us, he looked up and continued, "Your shield is your mind on the streets. There ain't nothing worse than being locked up like an animal. They make it like that on purpose. Rikers is more rough than upstate. They make sure that it's a place where you don't want to return."

I asked what he had learned about himself while being in the program, and he said, "I learned how to calm my temper. I was real hot-headed before. Now I know how to think about the consequences of my actions. I know how to be a man more than being a boy."

By providing mental health services, Brooklyn Adolescent Link went beyond mere issues of peer pressure or anti-social behavior, and dealt with issues that could not be corrected in a carceral environment. For many of their clients, they are providing a structure that they have never had. Rather than rehabilitation, they provide basic *habilitation*. The network of services provides insight to the needs of children in poor neighborhoods in general. With more programs like this, the criminal justice system may be able to make the necessary adjustments to preventing the predictable nature of adolescent recidivism rates.

Notes

1. Correctional Association of New York. "Each One Teach One." Retrieved from web site June 2, 2008: www.correctionalassociation.org/JJP/EOTO/EOTO.htm
2. Freire, Paulo. *Pedagogy of the Oppressed* (30th Anniversary edition). New York, N.Y.: The Continuum International Books, 2000.
3. Obtained from Correctional Association of New York webpage on July 3, 2006: http://www.correctionalassociation.org/JJP/index.htm
4. Scheer, Rebecca. "Keeping Track of New York City's Children: Status Report 2010." New York, N.Y.: Citizens' Committee for Children of New York, Inc., 2010.
5. Scheer, p. 165.
6. Arthur Pearl. "Cultural and Accumulated Environmental Deficit Models." from *The Evolution of Deficit Thinking: Educational Thought and Practice.* New York, N.Y.: Falmer Press, 1997.
7. G. Honor Fagan. *Culture, Politics and Irish School Dropouts.* New York, N.Y.: Greenwood Publishing Group, 1995.
8. Lewis, Oscar. *The Culture of Poverty.* New York, N.Y.: W.H. Freeman, 1966.
9. John Taylor Gatto. *The Underground History of American Education* (Oxford, U.K.: Oxford University Press, 2001).
10. Michel Foucault. "Structuralism and Structures of Knowledge." *Power: Essential Works of Foucault, 1954-1984: Volume 3.* New York: The New Press, 1994/1970.
11. Jonathan Kozol. *Savage Inequalities: Children in American Schools.* New York: Crown Publishers, 1991.
12. Robert K. Merton. "Opportunity Structure." *On Social Structure and Science.* Chicago, Ill.: University of Chicago Press, 1996.
13. Dewey, John. *Democracy and Education: An Introduction to the Philosophy of Education.* New York, N.Y.: The Macmillan Company, 1916.
14. Frederick, B. (1999). *Factors Contributing to Recidivism Among Youth Placed with New York State Division for Youth* (Research Report, State of New York Criminal Justice Services). Retrieved from Criminal Justice Services website August 3, 2010: http://www.criminaljustice.state.ny.us/crimnet/ojsa/dfy/dfy_research_
15. Butterfield, F. (July 12, 1999). "Prisons Brim With Mentally Ill, Study Finds." *NY Times*. P. A2.
16. Education and Assistance Corporation. Retrieved from website on January 24, 2007: website- http://www.eacinc.org/p-brklnadolfore.htm

17. Buck, Jeff, and Tami Mark. "Youths with Serious Emotional Disturbance: Date from the National Health Interview Survey" *Psychiatric Services.* 57:1573, November, 2006.

18. U.S. Department of Justice. "Juvenile Offenders and Victims: 2006 National Report." Retrieved on March 17, 2008 from Office of Justice Programs website: http://www.ojjdp.gov/ojstatbb/nr2006/index.html

19. Sasha, S.M. "Morbidity in the Ghettos during the Holocaust." *Harefuah, 141(4), April 2002.*

20. Scheer, p. 127.

21. Wilson, William J & Loic Wacquant. "The Ghetto Underclass and the Changing Structure of Urban Poverty," from *Quiet Riots: Race and Poverty in the United States.* Westminster, Md.: Random House, 1988.

22. United States Federal Bureau of Investigation. *Uniform Crime Report* (2008). Retrieved from FBI website: http://www.fbi.gov/ucr/ucr.htm#cius.

23. In any given year, the neighborhoods of East New York and Brownsville typically have the highest rates of violent crime in the city.

24. Lanier, Mark & Stuart Henry. *Essential Criminology, 2nd Edition.* New York, N.Y.: Westview Press, 2004.

Chapter 8: Disavowing Deprivation: Teens and Personal Responsibility

After hundreds of hours of qualitative research with the four chosen ATI programs, the theme of "choice" continued to surface over and over again. Could youth simply avoid the pitfalls of the juvenile justice system by *choosing* not to engage in crime? Was it as simple as "wising up?" Among all of the interviews I conducted with teenagers, a pattern emerged between the boys and girls. Whereas many of the boys spoke about the pressure to live up to expectations of Black or Latino masculinity, the young girls expressed having more options. Young boys represent 89 percent of all adolescent offenders, which suggests there is something different about boys in the choices they make.

Ronald Simons, Martin Miller, and Stephen Aigner (1980) suggested that the disproportionate amount of delinquent boys was due in part to being "differentially exposed."[1] This idea postulates that young boys commit more crimes because they have greater access to criminal activity. On the contrary, girls exhibit more pro-social behavior because they "come home on time for curfew," they "do their homework," and "they walk away when they sense trouble." Although there may be an ample amount of evidence to support this claim, it could be outdated. Young girls in deprived neighborhoods appear to be embedded in the same environments as their male counterparts, but their behavioral expectations differ.

In June 2008, I sat down with Jessica, a former participant of the Each One Teach One Youth Leadership Training Program. At eighteen, she was a recent graduate of Bronx Academy High School and a current resident of the Kingsbridge neighborhood in the West Bronx. Even though her neighborhood had one of the highest crime rates in the city, she felt safe and endearingly referred to her neighborhood as "little Dominican Republic." I asked her about the differences between boys and girls, and she thought it had a lot to do with cultural opportunity and peer pressure, although she had been equally exposed to some of the more negative aspects of street life.

Very casually, Jessica explained the frequency of violence in her neighborhood. Sitting in a café immediately below the train tracks of the number 1 train, she smirked as she reiterated, "Like three summers ago, a lot of teenage boys in the Bronx had died. So when it came to cookouts and outdoor stuff, everyone would know there that there was going to be a shootout. Either the person that killed a boy is going to come shoot it up, or somebody has been drinking or smoking too much, and now something is going to happen."

Violence to her was a norm, something that could be avoided if one stayed in his/her home. Or it was something to be dealt with when venturing outside of the home. She went on to explain, "There was one night I was hanging out with my cousin, and I have never seen so many police officers in my life. In the middle of the neighborhood. It wasn't even that late. And they just ran this one boy off his bike . . . And the police was telling us to get off the corner because they have stickups every weekend." Jessica sighed with the sad memories. "It's like every time I go out I'm running from somebody shooting, or like . . ." She sat up and her eyes widened, "I've had bullets fly past my head. I remember this one kid had an Uzi. And I didn't think they sounded like that!" She began chopping her hands past her ears. "Like *Pyoon! Pyoon! Pyoon! Pyoon! Pyoon! Pyoon! Pyoon!* And they were passing my ear as I was running. And it's just like . . ." Slumping back into her seat, "I don't know. And people still go to these cookouts."

"So you stopped going then?" I asked.

"Oh, no! Sometimes I'll go. And I'll leave real early. But sometimes people be like, *Oh no. This one won't be a shootout.* And they get shot anyway. And it's just like ridiculous. It's horrible. People are dying . . ." She gazed out of the café window, "It's corny to me. You know, the girls get really dressed up. The boys do too. But for what? I mean, you're putting on high heels and dresses just so you can run!"

"So you have to bring running shoes," I joked.

"Yeah, you know. I'm putting on my sandals. And it's just gets so sickening. I mean, every second someone has to argue. Like *Oh you looked at my girl. You stepped on my sneaker.* Like, *What the F you looking at?* And it's just so corny and young. And I'm young, but you guys are like twenty and twenty-one and this is what you do with your Saturdays?" Even though she spoke about her own friends, Jessica's disappointment was prominent. "We can't do anything anymore. You say you get mad when people are like *well, Black people are this way and that way.* You get mad, but then you do it! Shoot at each other and kill each other. What are you doing to prove the opposite, right?"

Jessica has expressed the frustration of many young girls growing up in a disadvantaged neighborhood. It was easy for her to grasp the logic behind personal responsibility. She understood that many young boys could stop themselves from getting into trouble, but she was also aware of the effects of her neighborhood's opportunity structure: "I just feel like . . . if you really gave people opportunities . . . Not that opportunities aren't around. But if you *gave* them opportunities, then they would act more different than they are now."

Jessica's perspective was shaped by her particular status in her neighborhood. She is very accomplished. She graduated from one of the top area high schools in the city. She has plans for college and has done an ample amount of volunteer work in youth programs. She is what is known is deprived neighborhoods as a "good girl" or a "ghetto nerd." This label comes with its own protections and expectations from everyone around her. Residents in the deprived dozen recognize that not many community members are destined to achieve greatness, so they put a lot of support and resources behind youth with promise. Jessica explained, "They care. People have these ideas about these boys and these girls that are from the hood . . . so called. And they care a lot about people who they do see have futures." Jessica began to blush, "I mean, they won't let me smoke a cigarette, as opposed to a regular girl if they see her smoking a cigarette. They won't let me drink . . . I mean, kids who grew up without fathers or without parents are *more* caring about their friends. Because they grew up with their friends."

The "ghetto nerd" is a real status and something that is familiar to those growing up in the deprived dozen. Hip Hop artist Mos Def claims to have been a ghetto nerd. Growing up in Bedford-Stuyvesant, he never engaged in the criminal trades, but instead chose to read and play indoors. This allowed him to become a successful college-student, musician, and eventually a Broadway actor. This is a status that is respected in deprived neighborhoods if one shows potential for success, or more honestly, potential to "get out of the ghetto." Gang members may provide protection for their high achieving little brothers. A dealer on the corner might look out for a "smart girl." Neighborhood elders may pool their resources behind a young kid with athletic talent.

The protected status of "those who have futures" is mostly afforded to young girls, and may partially explain the gender disparity in the juvenile justice system. But this does not mean that the choice to be "good" is not available to boys. Throughout many of my interviews with both boys and girls, many reiterated that girls have the option to parade through their neighborhoods with a good report card because that is what is expected of them. This may have its roots in the ethos of working class culture, which for generations has emphasized academic success for one's daughters and job success for one's sons. Adolescent girls raised in working class or working poor families have a very clear mandate laid out before them: *get 'As' or get in trouble*. For young boys, the message is a less candid: *prepare yourself to make money* (as this will fulfill your duties as a man to your family). One way of preparing oneself to earn a family wage is to complete high school, then go on to college to earn the credentials for a career. But many high school age boys see themselves in limbo as they contemplate to bypass the school route in order to earn money immediately.

Jessica had brought up an important point: that if society would *give* young boys opportunities, then they would see money-making schemes through more legitimate routes. But New York State officials do believe that they are doing everything they can for the troubled youth, but it is up to the youth to take some initiative. Many adults may see adolescents as lazy and arrogant; while teens look at adults in official positions as hostile and apathetic to their concerns. If the structure of juvenile justice is to change, then they may just have to meet halfway.

The Politics of Being Tough

Considering the "tough on crime" politics that dominate New York state criminal justice legislation, policy makers have been slow to acknowledge the worth of ATI programs. The average voting constituent tends to view a community-based program as something that leaves the potential for criminal activity right at their doorstep. Prisons, on the other hand, act as institutions of displacement, removing the agent of crime far from their neighborhood. The belief is that crime rates are at historic lows because all of the potential criminals have been locked away. An ATI program would only allow more opportunities for continued victimization. Therefore, New York state senators and assemblypersons have been responding to this belief by continuing to push legislation that increases punishments for juveniles.

Law-abiding residents of New York City tend to rely on the stereotypes of African American and Latino youth and adjust their behavior accordingly: by avoiding certain neighborhoods, switching train cars if it becomes too crowded with teens after school hours, or crossing the street if they see a group of teens approaching. A criminal justice system that allows wanton youth to freely roam the streets makes the average person uneasy. If teens are committing crimes, community members would prefer to have them placed *outside* of their communities.

Beginning with the Juvenile Offender Act of 1978, legislators have ignored the monetary value of ATI programs and instead have pushed for greater perceived public safety. Even though juvenile arrests have decreased 28 percent since 1993, the number of youth entering secure detention has actually increased 60 percent.[2] The criminalization of youthful behavior has grown in popularity, leaving a large population of teens without a voice or a platform to discuss their concerns. With the right platform, a select few can speak for the concerns of many, creating what Charles Tilly (1995) would call a "repertoire of contention" or an "established way in which pairs of actors make and receive claims bearing on each other's interests."[3]

Large cultural and political change tends to begin with small movements. With the appearance of disadvantage, there tends to follow a social movement: a "sustained, organized challenge to existing authorities in the name of a deprived, excluded or wronged population." For youth who have to deal with the daily fatigue of racial profiling and Panopticon-like neighborhood supervision, some ATI programs can act as an outlet to speak for their affairs.

The Juvenile Justice Coalition—organized by the Correctional Association of New York—acts as an arm of ATI initiatives dedicated to policy reform, rather than providing services. As a part of my work with the Each One Teach One program, I discovered the Juvenile Justice Coalition and their efforts towards policy reform in New York. The coalition had more than fifty member organizations, including all of the ATI programs featured in this book.

The most important annual event for the Juvenile Justice Coalition was called "Advocacy Day": where select groups of ATI program directors, case managers *and* program participants travel to Albany (New York state's capital) to meet with state legislators in an effort to advance proposals that will positively affect at-risk youth in New York City. On a cold February morning in 2006, I traveled with the coalition to document some of their efforts. Each participant in the event received "advocacy training" at the Correctional Association of New York. They also received instructions for the particular proposals being campaigned for. The particular issues on the table were outlined in a packet given to all the participants of the day:

> *Proposal 1: Redirect Money From Costly Youth Jails to Community Based Alternatives.
>
> *Proposal 2: Support Legislation that Will End the Prosecution of Sexually Exploited Youth. (Already on the Assembly floor in the form of "The Safe Harbor for Exploited Children Act—Bill A.6597/S.4423)
>
> *Proposal 3: Support Legislation to Protect the Rights of LGBT Youth in the Juvenile Justice System. (Already on the Assembly floor in the form of the SAFETY Act—Bill A.6502)
>
> *Proposal 4: Create a Child Advocate's Office to Safeguard Incarcerated Youth from Abuse. (Already on the Assembly floor in the form of the Office of the Child Advocate—Bill A.6334)

I was a part of one team that consisted of one adult leader and three youth from the Each One Teach One program. We had arranged meetings with several legislators, but we were only able to meet with one Assemblyman from the Oneida region of New York. As the conversation unfolded, I began to understand why so many have pushed for juvenile justice reform. As we sat down to engage the first proposal, I asked the first question: "If I'm not mistaken, you have a lot of corrections and police experience. I'm just curious how you feel about corrections and whether or not you feel it actually works in . . . 'correcting kids.'"

The Assemblyman took a sip of his coffee and then leaned back in his chair, a sprawling view of downtown Albany behind him. "I think corrections works on two fronts: Number one, it takes the bad person off the street and makes the community safe. The number one job of the police officer and the Corrections Department is to take these people who have committed crimes against the public, who have caused public disruption, and put them someplace where the rest of the public is safe.

"Now, in the correctional community or atmosphere, if that person is going to be rehabilitated, it is up to the individual if they want to be rehabilitated or not—[to] take advantage of the educational programs, the counseling and everything that is offered to them. Because we offer to them a multitude of programs to help people turn their lives around so that when they come out they're a better person than when they went in." The assemblyman adjusted his glasses and leaned forward. "If that person does not want to take advantage of that and doesn't want to learn and doesn't want to expand, and comes back out onto the street with the same attitude as when they went in, or in some cases even a worse attitude depending on who they hook up with inside, there's nothing that you or I or anybody else is going to do about that. That's all you can offer. If they only take advantage of it, and go on, and come out, wonderful, then the system works. If they don't, I don't know what the heck we can do about it."

Squirming in her chair, Tanisha spoke in a higher volume than the assemblyman, "Well, I honestly believe that the system doesn't work because a lot of youth who, you know, go to jail end up back in jail."

The assemblyman turned his palms to the ceiling, "Right."

"Because they committed other crimes."

"Right. Because they didn't take advantage of the programs that they had offered to them." The assemblyman leaned further across his desk and pointed at Tanisha, "They didn't want to change. And they think that it's cool. . . . I was an undercover narc for eight years, okay, I lived on the streets. And they think it's cool to act that way. They think it's cool to hang out with *those* members. They think it's cool to do drugs. They think it's cool to run wild. Because that's what people like . . ." Waving his hands to his sides, "But that's *not* what people like."

Increasing her volume even more, Tanisha continued, "Well I kind of feel like, basically, if you keep sending the child to the corner their next time out, and they feel like every time they come out they continue to do the same thing."

Interrupting her, "Ever been to jail?"

"No, I've never been to jail, but if they . . ."

"Have you ever been to jail?" Pointing at another teen in the room, "You ever been to jail?" Pointing at the last youth, "You ever been to jail?" Pointing at me, "You ever been to jail? Well I've never been to jail. And guess what? We did it right!"

Tempers between the assemblyman and Tanisha began to flare, both moving closer to the edge of their seats as they tried to out-speak each other.

Tanisha began to dig her nails into her legs, "I know, but I'm saying . . ."

"And when our parents . . ."

"Well some people have done it wrong."

"Well, you can't . . ."

"And when somebody does something wrong, you have to change something."

The assemblyman smacked the top of his desk, "That's right! And that's what I said. You put them in there. You give them the opportunities to change."

"You give them education. You give them counseling. You give them everything that they need. You give them medical; whatever it is. If they don't want to take advantage of it, and they come out as bad as they were when they went in, or worse, that's not your fault, it's not my fault, it's their fault! It's *their* fault! And people have to be responsible for their own actions. We will help you. But if you refuse the help, and don't want to take advantage of it, then that's *your* fault. And you will go back to jail."

Tanisha took in a small amount of air and exhaled slowly, "But what about some of the people? A certain percentage are not violent, they aren't taking some of the opportunities because they are removing them. If 76 percent . . ."

The assemblyman leaned his chair back and folded his arms, "There's an old saying: you can take a horse to water . . . but you can't make him drink."

"I know, but if only 24 percent of them are . . ."

"Have you ever heard that statement?"

"Maybe they need some other opportunities . . ."

"Have you ever heard that statement?! You can bring a horse to water but you can't make him drink?"

Tanisha began to turn red in the face, ". . . but a lot of people..."

"So what are you supposed to do?"

"And they . . ." Smacking her lap with both hands, "Open up more alternative centers!"

The assemblyman continued, "Put the horse's face down and force feed him water?"

"No. I just told you . . ."

"You just give him the opportunity. It's the same way with people."

With the conversation noticeably out of control, the adult leader—a reverend from a Brooklyn-based girls group—steered it in another direction, "I want to go back to something you just said. You sort of stopped to say that you don't want to categorize all people as bad. What if you have put a kid in placement who, for whatever number of reasons, may have been in the wrong place at the wrong time?

The assemblyman began pointing, "No."

The middle-aged reverend calmly adjusted her glasses and continued, "Some youth have developed the character of bad behavior, but have done nothing wrong. So looking at a young person like that, what we're suggesting here perhaps instead of incarcerating that youth for a first offense, so to speak."

"Nobody goes to jail for their first offense unless it's major."

"Exactly."

"I don't buy that story. I've done it enough times."

"But what we're saying . . ."

After taking another sip from his coffee, he continued, "They didn't learn when they went through the juvenile courts. They didn't learn when they went through counseling."

Continuing to sit up straight in her chair, the reverend reiterated, "What we're saying is, that for the sake of rehabilitation, we're not talking about a young person that has committed a capital crime. What we're saying is, if the cost is going to be one hundred and forty thousand dollars or one hundred and fifty thousand dollars to incarcerate that young person, essentially, perhaps to go in and get worse, *or* you could spend twelve thousand dollars . . ."

The assemblyman leaned further back in his chair to exaggerate his disbelief, "Twelve thousand? What are you saying costs twelve thousand dollars to rehabilitate somebody?"

"But we've already done that! They've done that. You can't put the kid in jail the first time he's committed a crime unless it's a major crime. Right?"

Even though my main objective was to be an observer, I felt it my duty to add some substance to the argument, "But that money is to . . ."

He continued without listening, "I knew an individual I locked up four times for selling narcotics. FOUR times. Alright? Did a year in the county jail, got out, BOOM, I copped him again. Went back in, they gave him another year in the county jail, until all the programs came up, BOOM, copped him again. Did two and half years state time, BOOM, copped him again. Finally, I knew the father. The father was a professional person in my area. And I said, *we got to do something with this kid. He's going to get killed, first of all*. And we took him aside and said, *You know, it's time that you got a set of brains*. Guess what? He's got a family. Four kids. Great job. He's involved with the community now. Because he finally learned. He *wanted to learn*. But if he didn't want to learn, like some of his buddies, BOOM, you go back again. That's the nature of things. You can't change everybody."

Tanisha interjected, "But only a small percent of those who go to alternative programs end up going back."

"Thirty percent, right?"

I included, "Thirty is the high end, for that matter."

The assemblyman smirked, "Alright so it worked for that thirty percent."

"No, it works for seventy percent," I clarified.

At this moment the phone rang, and the assemblyman answered without hesitation, "Hello? You got this . . . yeah okay." He hung up the phone and pointed indiscriminately towards the group, "I wasn't just a police officer walking around with blinders. I lived on the streets for eight years undercover."

I calmly clasped my hands together, "Sir, if I may just ask one more question. You mentioned about not taking advantage of help. You were saying that they, OCFS, provides tools for them to rehabilitate themselves."

"Of course they do. Everyone . . ."

"So all we're doing is comparing those that go to Corrections . . . These are for the same crimes. Let's say, rob one. [robbery in the first degree] . . . or something like that. 76 percent that go to OCFS commit crimes again. 76 percent that go to ATI programs do NOT commit crimes again. So I'm saying that . . ."

"Aaaahhh." Shaking his head, "I don't believe those numbers."

I sat up in my chair, "Those are real numbers! That's as reported by OCFS."

The assemblyman stood up and faced the door to the side of his desk, "That's fine. But I have to go now." He quickly shook hands with everyone and exited the room.

His staff assistant—who had been quietly standing in the back corner of the room—blushed slightly before debriefing us. "He's fired up about something else. He was probably just having a hard time. But he tends to get fired up over these issues." Walking towards us with her hand extended, she motioned for the door behind her, "And we just had an officer who just got shot in our town yesterday on a robbery. We're not used to crime like you. We just had a major crime clip. . . . I can sit down with him in another moment today and discuss it with him. When he's not in a rush." Just as fast as we came in, we exited the room, not sure of what had been accomplished.

Disavowing Cultural Deprivation

After the conversation with the New York assemblyman, the divide between disenfranchised urban youth and the upstate representatives was never more palpable. For legislators creating the template for juvenile justice, an institution of corrections is viewed as a reliable place for reform. As the assemblyman said, "You give them the opportunities to change . . . If they don't want to take advantage of it . . . It's *their* fault!" All of the tools for survival (and readjustment to the community) are designed to be located inside of the correctional facilities, therefore, advocacy to move money away from these facilities and putting them in the community may seem redundant.

At work in legislators' decision-making processes are their perceptions of young people, specifically young people of color. According to the Correctional Association of New York, "While African Americans and Latinos make up less than two-thirds of the city's youth population, they comprise 95 percent of the young people entering detention."[4] With such a large representation in correctional facilities, many view this as a cultural problem, a deficiency in Black and Latino culture in the socialization of law-abiding citizens. African American and Latino youth are expected to do worse in school, take the lowest rungs of the job market, and eventually find themselves in the carceral system because of the failures of their families and cultural norms. These youth are faced with the double-challenge of navigating poor social conditions in order to succeed and to disavow the expectations of cultural deficiency.

Although the achievement gap between African Americans and whites has changed significantly since the 1950s, the expectations of cultural failings for poor African Americans (and more recently Latinos) has not changed. Over the past few decades, any academic or journalistic discussion of poor African Americans often includes the words "crisis," "troubled," or in some cases, "endangered." In particular, there is a concern about *young Black and Latino men* and their inability to adapt to a changing society (whereas African American and Latina women are notably closing the achievement gap). Eric Eckholm (2006) of *The New York Times* wrote that "the huge pool of poorly educated black men are becoming ever more disconnected from the mainstream society."[5] The discourse on young African American and Latino males is often centered on the cultures' maladjusted notions of masculinity and how it relates to the social failure.

Particularly for young African American and Latino males—who face social exclusion in education, the criminal justice system, and are less accepted than women in the growing services economy—are confronted by diminished choices if the attempt to operate on older modes of patriarchal masculinity. When there is reduced access to traditionally masculine jobs, young men are being forced to reinvent themselves and some are having a difficult time doing so.

In a roundtable discussion with a group teens at the Each One Teach One program, I asked what type of profession they wanted to pursue as adults. There were eight girls and three boys present. The girls chose goals that either fit the professional or services economies, including "doctor," "lawyer," "psychiatrist," and "nurse." The girls seemed to be aware of the choices the economy had to offer. But there was recognition that these were competitive fields, so they needed to "stay in school" even if it wasn't the best quality.

The boys on the other hand—who had been raised on working class expectations to enter the working world as early as possible—dreamed about fields that led to fast wealth, but they were unsure how to go about achieving them. All of them wanted to be either a "music producer," a "professional basketball player," or—as the last boy explained—"I can't tell you that here. Not now." These young boys were struggling to find their place in a working lacking masculine choices.

The benefits of industrial patriarchy are rapidly becoming *disadvantages* in a post-industrialized global economy. According to Pierre Bourdieu (1998), "Male privilege is also a trap, and it has its negative side in the permanent tension and contention, sometimes verging on the absurd, imposed on every man by the duty to assert his manliness in all circumstances."[6] Machismo, hypersexuality, violence and patriarchal family structures are all denigrating to African American and Latino communities. The task of young men is to put these cultural notions aside and create *new stereotypes* for achievement.

For the young men involved with the Juvenile Justice Coalition, their efforts at changing the expectations of a deprived culture have been directed at policy makers and at middle-class blacks and Latinos alike. As is said by Mark Anthony Neal in *New Black Man* (2005):

> Although I'll be the first to admit the need to shepherd a generation of under-achieving, under-prepared, under-appreciative black male youth into a twenty-first century black manhood, I contend that a crisis of black masculinity exists not only in the scapegoated, so-called hip hop generation, but in the legions of well-adjusted, middle-classed, educated, heterosexual black men, whose continued investment in a powerful American-style patriarchy (often remixed as

> Black Nationalism and Afrocentrism) and its offspring homophobia, sexism, and misogyny, represents a significant threat to the stability and sustenance of black families, communities, and relationships.[7]

Young men have a struggle ahead of them to be more readily accepted into mainstream society. Young women of color have the same struggle, but are offered more protectionism and less pressure by their peers if they choose to be "good." ATI programs and their efforts to focus on social, as well as cultural issues, have paid off amongst their participants. Many of the programs featured in this book have offered young boys a new type of manhood and more choices, as was said by Felix of EOTO: "I learned that manhood should involve keeping the balance. Balance between working, schooling by choice and independence."

Advocacy Day provided a means to dispel the notions of cultural deprivation while advocating to change the structures that affect young urbanites in disadvantaged communities. Upstate legislators might look at youth from New York City's deprived dozen as lazy and complacent, but their advocacy proved otherwise. At the end of the day, all of the team members reconvened in an assembly hall in the state building to debrief. Each team took turns speaking of their successes and failures. In between, a familial atmosphere descended on the audience. Felix in particular approached me to ask, "How did it go? Did everything go well?" Like many of the others, his posturing was more communal. One ATI group led the coalition in chants of "No Justice! No Peace!" and "No More Youth Jails!" The day ended with EOTO youth coordinator Assadullah Muhammad leading everyone in a "one word circle" where everyone was allowed one word to sum up their feelings of the day. All one-hundred team members held hands and spoke of "empowerment," "frustration," and "family." Their communal efforts did eventually pay off with the passing of the Office of the Child Advocate Bill a couple of months later.

Notes

1. Simons, Ronald, I., Martin G. Miller, and Stephen M. Aigner (1980). "Contemporary Theories of Deviance and Female Delinquency: An Empirical Test." *Journal of Research in Crime and Delinquency.* 17: 42-57.

2. Correctional Association of New York. "Rethinking Juvenile Detention in New York City" Produced on March 2002. Retrieved from website on April 21, 2005: http://www.correctionalassociation.org/publications/download/jjp/rethinking_detention.pdf.

3. Tilly, Charles. "Contentious Repertoires in Great Britain." from Traugott, Mark (editor). *Repertoires & Cycles of Collective Action.* London: Duke University, 1995.

4. Correctional Association of New York., p. 3.

5. Eckholm, Eric. (March 20, 2006). "Plight Deepens for Black Men, Studies Warn." *New York Times.*

6. Bourdieu, Pierre. *Masculine Domination.* Stanford, Calif.: Stanford University, 1998.

7. Neal, Mark Anthony. *New Black Man.* New York, N.Y.: Routledge Press, 2005.

Chapter 9: The Survival Kit at Work

As I approached the front entrance of Daniel Webster Houses in the South Bronx, four young men in their early twenties seated on a nearby bench brought their conversation to a complete halt. All four stared intently; one stood and started to slink his way towards the court yard between two buildings. Another grabbed his arm, "Naw, son. He ain't police. Chill." I glanced and gave a quick nod as I reached for the call panel by the front door. Their expressions didn't as the door buzzed and I was in within seconds.

After walking across the hall I entered the elevator, en route to the eighteenth floor. The intoxicating smell of urine forced me to tuck the bottom half of my face into my jacket as I contemplated my goal for the day: after months of trying to get a hold of him, I was going to interview Antoine. A former participant of BronxConnect, he later explained that he was avoiding me because he thought I was "someone in the Probation Department looking to violate me."

After two years of sitting inside and observing ATI programs, I wondered if they were effective. Did they provide the tools necessary to guide these young people to live a crime-free lifestyle? Were they being taught how to survive? Or had I been fooling myself into thinking that ATI programs provide a survival kit that is not available elsewhere in the criminal justice system? Two years removed from the program, Antoine was one of several former clients that I set out to interview in order to measure their *quality of life*.

As the elevator opened, I made my way down the hall and knocked at the far door. Greeting me at the door was a smiling Antoine, who invited me inside. As we walked towards his bedroom, I noticed a middle-aged woman frying something up in the kitchen as a small child played with blocks by her feet. Antoine's bedroom was small. A mattress on the floor dominated most of the space. His walls were covered with posters of famous Hip Hop acts, some amateur graffiti, and a couple of small holes that could have been made by his fists. A large chunk of wallpaper had been partially torn down and then covered by another poster. A few stick figures drawn by a child's hand nestled in the wall space above his bed pillow. I glanced out of the window and took in the distant view of Claremont Park as he cleared a nearby desk chair and then invited me to sit.

After setting up my tape recorder and notebook, I asked him some basic questions. "Before you went to BronxConnect, what was your original charge?" Settling himself on the edge of his mattress, Antoine began to explain, "A fight in school. I had a fight with some boy. I ain't never seen the boy again. The teacher asked me to go downstairs and get a newspaper." Illustrating the space between him and the boy with his hands, "I had walked past this boy and he was staring at me. And I don't even know who he was. I walked past him, and then he said something, and all of a sudden we was fighting." Oddly enough after his arrest, he was arraigned and charged with a second degree robbery charge, even though Antoine claimed, "I never took nothing from him." But it was this charge that brought him into the criminal justice system and in contact with the Bronx-Connect program.

Antoine had been born and raised in the Claremont Village neighborhood of the South Bronx, and he spent his entire life dealing with the difficulties of living in Webster Houses. From a young age, he had to earn an ample amount of violent capital and a reputation for having a short fuse. Claremont Village is one of the poorest areas of the city with disproportionately high violent crime rates. Webster Houses in particular has a reputation for being dangerous. When I asked him if his neighborhood was safe, he laughed and replied, "Naw!"

"Well, what's wrong with it?"

"There's always something going wrong. People getting killed, robbed, shot. Everybody wants to be your friend, and then they just turn against you." He glanced over his shoulder out of his bedroom window, "You got to be by yourself on this block. . . . Just stay away. Don't involve yourself in other people's nonsense."

"What is it about this neighborhood that might cause high crime rates?"

Shifting his weight on his bed, Antoine continued, "I say because we don't got a lot of programs after school anymore. Before we used to have programs after school; basketball games; we had a gym to go to. Now it's like, there's nothing to do. So some people just *don't got it*, and they do what they have to do to *get it*. Some people over here like to just do it [crimes], just to do it. Some people want to be tough . . . that's basically it. It all depends on what you want to do. You can hang out with a group of people over here, and they always be robbing people."

As the interview progressed, I could sense that Antoine felt isolated from his community. In general, he felt that socially acceptable modes for being a young man only included the ability to attain money quickly and stand your ground if ever confronted with violence. These were choices that he no longer felt were viable. He explained that some involve themselves in robberies in order to survive until the next day, while others do it for reputation, "Some people, they want to be down. They want people to know them as someone who do stuff like that." He began to shake his head, "But everybody do they own thing. Everybody got they own rep. Some people want their rep to be up there so they do mad stuff, so everybody know what they do." Flipping his hands into the air, "They think it's cute to go to jail, come out, like . . . I see it as, you go to jail, people that claim that they're your friends. . . . The only ones that's the real ones is the ones that come see you in jail. I see a lot of people go to jail, but I don't see nobody go see none of them."

I probed further, "Do you think people are afraid to go to jail?"

"Honestly, I know *I* was afraid at first. But then, after that, I was like, *if it happens it happens.* I can't do nothing about it. Some people just do it to do it, and they don't think about the consequences. . . . When people go to jail, they be scared in there because they be getting beat up. But you can tell, on the block, for a person that really don't want to go back, they not going to do it again. If they don't care, then they going to keep doing what they do over there."

Antoine was very familiar with the code: jail time was a norm for some of the young boys in his neighborhood. It was something that a handful of the children in his building looked forward to. So many had come back from completing a jail sentence, only to speak about it as if it were something that was tolerable. Antoine shook his head, "You supposed to talk to [children] about it like, *naw, its not even worth it. You being away from home, you being sent away . . . naw.* You'd rather have a roof over your head rather than asking someone if you can use the bathroom, or eat. That's not me."

As a result of his robbery charge, Antoine had spent time both in Rikers Island Correctional Facility and Spofford Juvenile Detention Center. Jail was something that he never wanted to revisit, and therefore took advantage of his time in BronxConnect. I asked about some of the special services he received: "When you first came to BronxConnect, what were some of the issues that needed to be addressed in your life?"

"At that particular moment, I think I needed to control my anger. To be more of an open person, because I tended to keep everything inside." Antoine attended regular anger management courses, which he believed paid off. "Before, I was more hot headed. I really wouldn't care. You know? You mess with me, I would fight you. Now, I get to that point, but then I think about it like, *Alright if I fight him, he might call the cops and then I'll be in jail again.* Now I just think about it. And I stop and walk away."

"Did you have some sort of turning point while you were in the program that led you to where you are today?"

Glancing towards his bedroom door and then back at me, "Yeah. I got a son now. So now I have to be that older person . . . because I know he's going to look up to me." Antoine smiled, "Everyday I look at him and he try to do things that I do . . . I want him to be a better person. I just don't want him to do nothing dumb. I want him to think about it before he do it. That's what I never used to do. I used to never think, I just did."

"So what do you do now to stay out of trouble."

"I got some friends who be like, *yo, let's go rob somebody.* And I'm like, *Naw, I'm good. Y'all go do what you want to do. I'm not going back to jail be-*

cause y'all want to go catch some petty ten dollars or something. It's not even worth it. I would rather be broke than go back to jail."

At the moment, it was unclear whether it was the fear of imprisonment or the tools acquired in the program that encouraged him to remain crime-free for the previous two years. I asked about the effects of the program, "Do you believe your life would be better or worse if you had never been in the program?"

Without hesitation, Antoine answered, "It had been worse. I think I would be in jail right now . . . Right now. Because without that program, I would have been doing that eighteen months in Lincoln Hall. And I know in Lincoln Hall they let you do home visits. And I know I'm not the type of person that's going to want to come home and then go all the way back upstate. No, I would be running. I know myself, so I would just get more time. They I would have just kept going. I would have had nobody to help me or nothing."

Like many of the individuals that I interviewed, nineteen-year old Antoine appreciated what the program had given to him. Although he felt that he needed to isolate himself in order to stay of out trouble, he credited BronxConnect with providing him the insight to look beyond street life. He wanted to focus on raising his son, and one day starting his own business. Even though he wasn't the biggest fan of schooling, he recognized that he had to finish his high school equivalency and then attend college to obtain legitimate independence. Only time would tell if he could achieve his goals without falling victim to the circumstances that surrounded him.

The Effectiveness of ATI Programs for Youth

The big question for any criminal justice initiative is whether it actually increases public safety. One way of measuring public safety is by observing if there is any corresponding decrease in crime rates with the increase in usage of said initiative. Another way of measuring the effectiveness of a criminal justice initiative is by looking at ex-criminals: after traversing the mechanisms of the criminal justice initiative will the criminal offender commit new crimes? In criminology this is referred to as recidivism. Correctional facilities are designed to reform individual criminals, and therefore reduce recidivism rates. The same should be true for adolescents going to prison for their criminal offenses, but the question becomes: are our communities actually safer? Will former adolescent offenders be ready to live a crime-free lifestyle once they return to the community? And more relevant to this study: are ATI programs (as a criminal justice initiative) *more* effective at reducing recidivism rates?

Recidivism is an arbitrary concept. It literally translates to a "repeated or habitual relapse in criminal behavior,"[1] but there is debate over how to operationalize "relapse." Some criminal justice agencies measure recidivism by studying new arrests rates for ex-offenders, while others look at *indictments* (being charged in court), while others still look at *conviction* rates (receiving a sentence after being found guilty). The New York State Division of Criminal Justice Services claimed in 1999 that adolescent offenders had a 75 percent recidivism rate after their release from the Office of Children and Family Services (formally the Division for Youth); but this was only an indication of arrests after thirty-six months.[2] In fact, most agencies prefer this indicator for recidivism because NYPD keeps the most accurate and publicly accessible records of arrests.

For adolescent offenders, there are various reports measuring their recidivism rates. While the 1999 Division for Criminal Justice Services report concluded that 81 percent of males and 45 percent of females in New York State were rearrested within thirty-six months,[3] a new study by the Office of Children and Family Services (2009) claims that those numbers have risen to 89 percent for boys and 81 percent for girls.[4] Very few have looked at the recidivism rates of ATI programs, and virtually none have looked at ATI programs for youth. If ATI programs can be considered to be effective criminal justice initiatives that increase public safety, then they should be examined.

The New York City Criminal Justice Agency (a private research corporation) released a report in April 2003 looking at five ATI programs: The Center for Alternative Sentencing and Employment Services' Court Employment Project (CEP); Fortune Society's Freedom Program; Osborne Association's El Rio Day Treatment Program; Fortune Society's FlameTree Program; Fortune Society's DAMAS program; and the Project Return Foundation's Women's Day Treatment Program. Only one of these programs was an ATI serving youth (CEP—ages sixteen to nineteen), and three of them were substance abuse treatment programs. CJA's four data sets compared jail (typically used to pre-plea detention), prisons (post-adjudication), probation (post-adjudication) and ATI programs. The study "found no significant difference among felony-ATI participants and felons serving a probationary sentence or felons released from state prison. However, the ATI group was more systematically less likely to recidivate than a similar group of offenders discharged from City jail."[5]

A similar study by the Vera Institute of Justice (a non-profit policy research organization) in 2001 focused exclusively on ATI programs. This report examined nine programs, including: Freedom, Crossroads (both general population and women's group), El Rio, Flametree, Project Return, DAMAS, Hopper Home, the Court Employment Project (CEP), and the Center for Community Alternative's Youth Advocacy Project (YAP). Two of these programs were for youth (CEP and YAP). Although this report examined the mechanics of ATIs as whole, it had a section dedicated the measurement of re-arrests *and* dispositions (convictions and case dismissals). The Vera Institute defined recidivism as "being arrested for a crime that occurred on or after the day a defendant was admitted to a study ATI."[6] Their report concluded that "being in an ATI program was not significantly associated with being more likely to survive over two years with a new arrest" considering age, offense, and where the defendant was being prosecuted. Yet *completing* an ATI program "strongly and significantly reduced the likelihood of rearrest." There were no definitive statements made about the youth programs, and here is where I found the missing link in my research.

There has been no significant research done on the recidivism rates (arrests, indictments, or convictions) for ATI programs that exclusively serve adolescents. Although the Juvenile Justice Project of the Correctional Association of New York claims that ATIs for juveniles have an 18-30 percent recidivism rate, these numbers are self-reported by the ATI programs themselves rather than being measured with any real empiricism.

Post-ATI Survival

After three years of ethnographic exploration of these programs, I wondered if this "kit" worked after youth completed the programs. Beginning in May 2007, I worked exclusively with the BronxConnect Youth Program to draft a quantitative study that would measure the effectiveness of the tools provided. I sought out to measure new arrest rates, new convictions rates, and to interview former participants in order to measure their "quality of life." For the purposes of this small study, a *crime-free lifestyle* indicates that an individual has not been arrested or acquired a new court conviction. *Effectiveness* is defined as living a crime-free lifestyle after program participation. *Recidivism* includes both new arrests and/or new criminal court convictions after a youth had initially had contact with the criminal justice system. These were measured by looking at the criminal histories of former program participants and other referrals to BronxConnect.[7]

I gathered and analyzed the criminal histories of 141 referrals to the program dated January 1, 2001 to December 31, 2004. The 141 referrals were then divided into three cohorts: (A) successful graduates of BronxConnect; (B) participants who served at least six months in the program but did not graduate or failed out of the program (i.e. for lack of participation and/or cooperation); and (C) Those who were incarcerated by the Office of Children and Family Services without any program contact. Another set of youth were lumped together and kept separate because they qualified for the program, but either had their cases dismissed, were found not-guilty, or were transferred to another program entirely.

The results of this study demonstrated that 64.5 percent of the youth who were outright incarcerated with OCFS (cohort C) had at least one new arrest within a year of their release from custody. 58.1 percent of these youth were convicted of a new offense. (See figure 9a.) After three years, 83.9 percent of the same set of youth had a new arrest and 77.4 percent were convicted of a new offense. (See figure 9b.) These numbers are consistent with the 1999 DCJS report and the 2009 OFCS report, which were essentially looking at the same population. But their numbers went up even further after five years of release from prison custody: 80.6 percent of those placed in OCFS had new convictions. (See figure 9c.) Overall, 68 percent of the youth originally placed in OCFS were convicted of new felony offenses—including mostly "possession of a controlled substance with intent to distribute" charges.

Figure 9a: Recidivism Rates One Year after Contact with Program or Incarceration

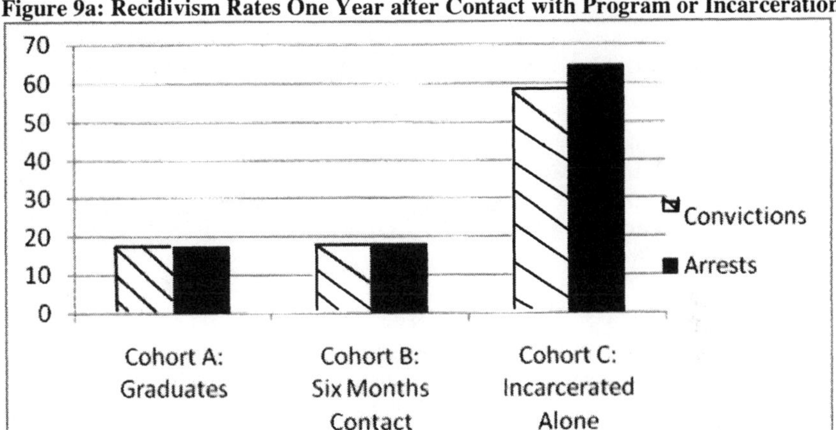

Youth mandated to participate in BronxConnect had significantly lower recidivism rates within a year of their exit from the program. Only 18.2 percent of those who served at least six months in the program but did not graduate (cohort B) were arrested for a new offense. (See figure 9a.) The same amount of cohort B was convicted of new offenses (18.2 percent). After three years, 72.7 percent of cohort B was arrested for a new offense, while 54.5 percent was convicted for a new offense. (See figure 9b.) After five years, 81.8 percent of cohort B was arrested for a new offense, but only 54.5 percent was convicted of a new offense. (See figure 9c.) More importantly, 50 percent of cohort B who had recidivated were convicted of misdemeanor charges.

The successful graduates (cohort A) had the best recidivism numbers of the entire study. Only 17.4 percent of the successful graduates of BronxConnect were arrested for a new offense (see figure 9a.) The same number of successful graduates were convicted of new offenses. Surprisingly, this matched up near perfect with the self-proclaimed numbers of the other ATI programs. After three years, 60.9 percent of the graduates of BronxConnect were arrested for a new offense, while 43.5 percent were convicted of a new offense [see figure 9b]. After five years, the gap between ATI participants and non-participants began to grow, but showed a significant difference in conviction rates: 73.9 percent of the graduates were arrested for a new offense, but only 47.8 percent were convicted of a new offense [see figure 9c]. More importantly, 74 percent of all the graduates who had recidivated were convicted of misdemeanor charges. More than half were for possession of marijuana alone.

The results demonstrate that 82.6 percent of former participants of BronxConnect were able to remain in their respective communities without any new arrests or new criminal activity for at least one year. For *all* of the youth who received services from BronxConnect, the first year after program completion

Figure 9b: Recidivism Three Years after Contact with Program or Incarceration

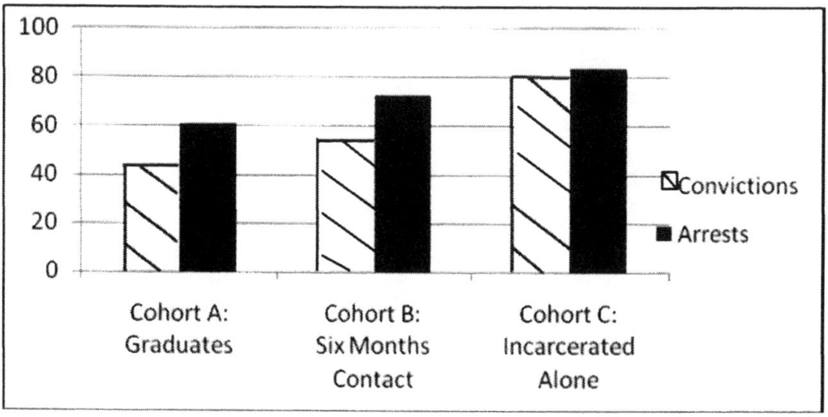

appeared to demonstrate the most effectiveness and provided the most evidence of an acquired skill set for living a crime-free lifestyle. Only 41.9 percent of youth released from OCFS were able to avoid a new arrest.

The difference between the youth who went to prison outright and those who participated in BronxConnect began to shrink as their contact with the program or prison approached the three-year mark. That margin shrank slightly more so at the five-year mark. Although the margin shrank, it's very important to note the differences in criminal activity. Whereas approximately 66 percent of every youth referred to the program initially committed felony offenses, the youth placed in OCFS continued in that trend by averaging four new convictions with a 68 percent felony conviction rate. In contrast, only 27 percent of the offenses of the graduates were for felonies, including "weapons possession," "assault," "robbery," and "sale of controlled substance." At an average of two new offenses over a five year period, the majority of the graduates convicted of a new offense committed misdemeanor charges, including "trespassing," "disorderly conduct," and "possession of small amounts of marijuana." This may be more of an indication of the conditions of their neighborhood environments than a continued criminal mindset.

Once the quantitative piece was completed, I set out to interview former participants of the BronxConnect Youth Program, the Each One Teach One Youth Leadership Training Program, and Brooklyn Adolescent Link. Being such a transient population, I was only able to interview ten former participants overall, but all provided interesting insights into the life after contact with the juvenile justice system. I was curious about their lifestyle choices, plans, how they were living and whether or not the ATI programs had made "any contributions to their life today." I preferred to interview them in their homes (when allowed) in order to observe the true nature of their current circumstances, combined with their self-reporting. For most, their place of residence did not change

Figure 9c: Recidivism Five Years after Contact with Program or Incarceration

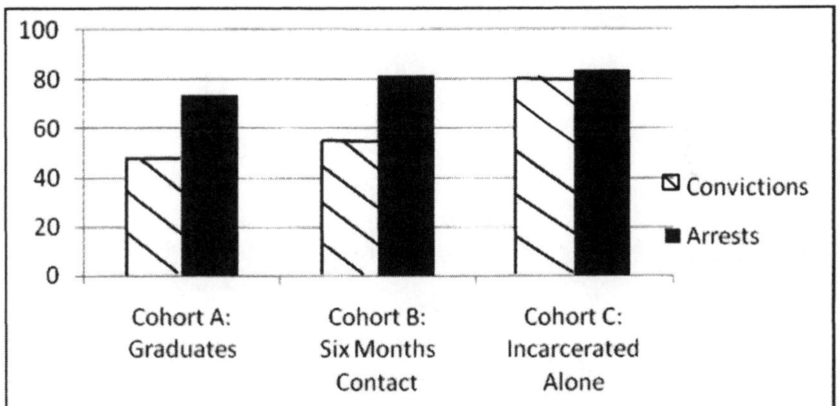

and therefore, they were dealing with the same social conditions from before their time in the ATI program. Most could better deal with these circumstances by using the advice and guidance provided to them by the program.

For one young man in particular, he had dedicated himself to complete lifestyle changes even though he lived in the same small apartment with his mother in the Mount Hope section of the Bronx. Randy's two-bedroom apartment was small and clean, warm feeling. This seemed worlds away from the litter, graffiti, and drunken old men in front of his building. Randy had originally been charged with "possession of an illegal firearm," something that could have earned him three years in prison, but he was instead able to complete his court-mandated program requirements and was halfway through his five year probation sentence.

When I asked Randy if his "life would be better or worse if [he] had not received services from BronxConnect?" he looked to his side to contemplate for a moment and then responded, "I would be worse. I would have never cared. Not caring about life—I have seen it in others. I have two friends that were arrested for new crimes and were sent upstate. One of them came home, and he didn't learn *anything*. Another came out and he is working now, but his dad's in jail."

Several of the clients of BronxConnect and Each One Teach One claimed that the programs were good at eliminating their idle time and "kept me out of trouble," but I wanted to know if they were effective at providing them tools for surviving in their neighborhoods after program contact. Did they walk away with something? Randy claimed that "If I see trouble coming, I walk away. Give my boys a pound and leave. If someone wants to be hard, *let him.* At least I didn't get murdered." He claimed that he used to have "a very short temper" and the program taught him to "be more calm."

I asked him if there was a "turning point" that led him to stay away from jail. Randy appeared proud of his changes. "I knew that I had to change. I don't want to be one of these dropouts out here without money. There are older men in his neighborhood who haven't done much with themselves are still living like teenagers. If I never went into the program, I wouldn't be like this. I'm more sober now, calm. I'm by myself. I don't hang out too much anymore."

Devin—another client of BronxConnect—claimed that he used be a part of "a big crew that was always into doing dumb stuff." He was originally charged with robbery in the first degree. In fact, he was somewhat of a "serial robber" that constantly "picked on people and plotted against strangers." But the program taught him to turn over a new leaf, "It was like karma for what I had done. I realized that people work hard for their money." Devin could have spent up to ten years in prison, but instead had remained crime-free for three years and had plans to move to Virginia to study computer programming.

Rianna—a participant of Each One Teach One and resident of South Jamaica, Queens—believed that the program had changed her. "I thought the program was going to be like 'scared straight.' Boring. But it turned out to be the opposite." Rianna had been charged with misdemeanor assault when the program was suggested to her. She had a penchant for fighting other young girls in her school and didn't concern herself too much with her future until she went to EOTO. "I realized that I like social activism. After I went to Albany for Advocacy Day, that changed my life." At the time of our interview, she was attending the State University of New York while majoring in political science.

Justin—a client of Brooklyn Adolescent Link—understood that he needed to address his mental health issues and to remove himself from some of the people he used to associate with: "Negative people. People who say they are friends, but they're not." Justin recognized one of the greatest detriments to a crime-free lifestyle was negative peer-influence, "[bad friendships] are like an anchor. You have to cut that chain and float to the top. . . . These are people who are not doing anything with themselves." He admitted that he would "probably still be robbing people" if he stayed in the same circles. He was more than appreciative for what Brooklyn Adolescent Link had done for him and he could readily list the tools that were provided to him, leading to a law-abiding outcome.

Many of the former ATI clients did not come from good backgrounds and were struggling with the dilapidated structures that were available to them. In some cases, even as former clients, the ATI remains the only viable support system that holds their survival together. Most of the participants I spoke with had let their ties with the ATI program fizzle, while some still maintained contact.

Being community-based programs, the former participants recognized the ATI as part of their community, a place where they can always seek advocacy.

When examining the "success" of an ATI program, just as important as measuring its recidivism rates is to measure the conditions and quality of life that lead to high rates of recidivism. Leading a crime-free lifestyle is in part a matter of individual will and personal choice, but this also assumes that all persons possess the right tools to make these choices. In the 1999 DCJS report, it was stated that over 95 percent of all recidivating juveniles "had problems in four or more of the following areas: mental health, substance abuse, behavior at school, academic performance, handicapping conditions, household characteristics, criminal or abusive family environment, or personal relationships with other family members."[8] Certainly for the remaining 5 percent, we can hold them personally accountable without any external intervention. For the majority, there needs to be something else in place to aid in creating a pro-social lifestyle.

Notes

1. "Definition of 'recidivism.'" Retrieved August 6, 2010 from dictionary.com website: http://dictionary.reference.com/browse/recidivism?fromRef=true

2. Frederick, B. (1999). *Factors Contributing to Recidivism among Youth Placed with New York State Division for Youth* (Research Report, State of New York Criminal Justice Services). Retrieved September 2, 2009 from Criminal Justice Services website: http://www.criminaljustice.state.ny.us/crimnet/ojsa/dfy/dfy_research_report.pdf

3. Frederick, p. 1.

4. Coleman, Rebecca, Susan Mitchel-Herzfeld, Do Han Kim, and Therese A. Shady. "Long-Term Consequences of Delinquency: Child Maltreatment and Crime in Early Adulthood." *Final Report.* Office of Children and Family Services. (commissioned by the U.S. Department of Justice: National Institute of Justice, March 31, 2009).

5. Savolainen, Jukka. "The Impact of Felony ATI Programs on Recidivism." Report by the Criminal Justice Agency: April, 2003.

6. The Vera Institute of Justice. "Balancing Punishment and Treatment: Alternatives to Incarceration in New York City." June, 2001. Retrieved March 2, 2005 from Vera Institute website: http://www.vera.org/download?file=75/Balancing%2BATI.pdf.

7. Funding for this study was provided by the Heckscher Foundation for Children, and the criminal histories were provided by the New York State Department of Criminal Justice Services.

8. Frederick, p. 2.

Epilogue: The Future of Juvenile Justice Reform

At times it is difficult for adults to empathize with crime-engaged teenagers. Oozing with conceit, loud in their clothing and their speaking volume, teenagers seem too confident and arrogant to warrant any "help." Most adults coast right into arguments about accountability and personal responsibility: "*When I was his age, my parents never would have let me leave the house with my underwear hanging out of my pants*." We have plenty of laws that criminalize adolescent deviant behavior: Florida's "sagging pants law," New York's arbitrary use of loitering and disorderly conduct statutes, and Hawaii's teen curfew laws, are examples. Teenagers act like they know it all, and often forget how misguided their behavior can be. We as adults tend to forget that we've all been there.

At sixteen years old I used to chase girls, smoke cigarettes in high school stairwells, and steal beer from local convenient stores with my friends. I, too, was a knucklehead. A completely different person then compared to now, I had very little concern for my future or the ripple effects of my actions in the present. I was lucky to have never been arrested.

Compared to adolescents in New York City, I was also tremendously lucky to have the life chances that led to my current status in life. I grew up in a two-parent working-class household in southeast Massachusetts. There was exceptional drug and alcohol consumption in my neighborhood, but it was kept indoors. My township had a wealthier tax base than the neighborhood I resided in, therefore, I attended a high school with well-paid teachers, up-to-date books, and great athletic and vocational programs. My opportunity structure kept me afloat as my negative adolescent impulses slowly dissolved into adulthood responsibility. I was lucky.

For teens growing up in the deprived dozen, not only do they have biological impulse stacked against them, but they also have to navigate an environment threatening to their safety. They are the most volatile demographic in our society: one with a social structure that filters them towards incarceration, and one with an incredible amount of social pressure on them to behave a certain way (especially for young boys). Take the recent story of seven Bronx teenagers who tortured and murdered another young boy and older man for allegedly engaging in homosexual sex.[1] The seven teens were members of the Latin Kings and discovered some behaviors that violated their conception of what man/boyhood should include. The unnamed seventeen year old victim had been punished for being who he truly was. Ironically, he was sodomized before being murdered by the boys who *condemned* the practice of sodomy.

Because of social pressure, subpar impulse control, impoverished institutional support, and swarming police supervision, teens in disadvantaged neighborhoods have an increased likelihood of violating the legal codes. Incarceration is only a temporary, stultifying solution to a worsening problem. The more that we warehouse children in institutions designed for the punishment of criminals, the more that we are preparing them for a criminal lifestyle as adults. What are we to expect from school-age kids serving time in prison except learning the ins and outs of the criminal trades?

For every adolescent entering the criminal justice system, there are always some biological factors to be considered, typically some family problems, and a pinch of cultural factors. Most cases involve a predictable recipe of structural conditions: poverty, poor education, single-parent homes and some mental or emotional health issues. These issues cannot be addressed strictly through confinement. If anything, adolescent offenders need *more* guidance, opportunity structure, and rehabilitative efforts than adult offenders, what I refer to as "Survival Kit Theory."

Survival Kit Theory refers to the distribution and accumulation of social tools necessary to facilitate sustainable living in a given social structure. Willpower or personal responsibility alone does not guarantee one's survival. You can be an excellent hunter, but it would be meaningless if there was no food to hunt. In post-industrial New York City, dedicated job-hunting is meaningless without plenty of living-wage jobs. Tireless scholarship is fruitless in a school designed for failure. But as I discovered throughout my research, where one resource is missing, others can be found. In this sense, the hunter can be taught to *gather* food.

The Survival Kit does not have to be provided by an ATI program. Young people can accumulate the necessary "tools" inside a dedicated household, school setting, or even a correctional facility. It depends on the goals and use of local knowledge by the distributive agent. In my case, I accumulated the necessary tools within the social structure of my upbringing. For "at-risk" youth in New York City, ATI programs tend to carry the load where family, high school and prison systems cannot (or will not).

The success of ATI programs seems in part due to their intentional focus on individual attention and cultural reconstruction. ATIs also allow the young person to utilize their newly acquired "tool kit" in the environment where it is most necessary. Juvenile prisons—originally called "training schools"—were designed to remove youth from their environment and to provide a survival kit to them in an institutional setting. Community-based programs are more effective today because youth are able to practice new survival skills where it matters most: their neighborhoods.

The juvenile justice system in New York City is beginning to shift more towards the medical model (as is evidenced in the Department of Juvenile Justice's merging with the Administration for Children's Services). This merging implies that crime-engaged children will be protected rather than punished. Prisons in general are overcrowded, and politicians are beginning to wise up to the ridiculously high recidivism rates in the adult and juvenile populations. Nationwide, the use of community justice is beginning to grow. Many criminal justice agencies prefer to lean on high-tech monitoring like GPS tracking of probationers or alcohol-monitoring ankle bracelets for those caught drinking and driving. But there is a small window open for grass-roots community-based programs that seek to rehabilitate youth through the social capital already available in the neighborhood.

In the near future, we may see a reverse of the trend that began in the early 1980s. Community residents feel safer with our historically high incarceration rates, but we now have an overwhelming amount of evidence that incarceration has little to no effect on deterrence. Diversion and community-based sanctions allow offenders to maintain ties in the community, learn the value of community reciprocity, and they provide law-abiding residents an opportunity for collective efficacy: a chance to personally engage in their own safety (especially through its younger members).

The criminalization of childhood will only be detrimental to our society in the long run. Teens are hardwired for study; sponges that absorb and internalize everything around them. If such retentive beings are placed in a total institution dedicated to warehousing society's most unwanted, that will do more for the complete socialization of a *criminal class* than it will do for anyone's public safety. Whether through ATI programs, residential institutions, or home settings, more effort needs to be made to train young people to survive as post-industrial utilitarians. Their survival has implications on us all.

Notes

1. Parascandola, R. and Siemasko, C. (Oct. 8, 2010). "7 from Bronx gang Latin Kings Goonies nabbed for brutal gay bash attack on man, 2 teens." New York Daily News:http://www.nydailynews.com/news/ny_crime/2010/10/08/2010-1008_7_from_bronx_gang_latin_king_goonies_nabbed_for_brutal_gay_bash_attack_on_man_2_.html

Bibliography

Abu-Lughod, Janet. *New York, Chicago, Los Angeles: America's Global Cities*. Minneapolis: University of Minnesota Press, 1999.

Amsden, David. (2006, April 9). "The One-Man Drug Company." *New York Magazine*. Retrieved from http://nymag.com/news/features/16653/.

Anderson, Elijah. "The Code of the Streets." *The Atlantic Monthly,* vol. 273, no. 5, 1994, pp. 81-94.

Anderson, Elijah. *Streetwise: Race, Class, and Change in an Urban Community*. Chica go: University of Chicago Press, 1990.

Appel, H. (2007, July 12). "Assaults, Murder on Kingsbridge Bring Increased Surveillance." Retrieved from Norwood News website on July 18, 2010: http://www.norwoodnews.org/story/?id=89&story=assaults,+murder+on+kingsbridge+bring+increased+surveillance.

Austin, James, Kelly Johnson, and Ronald Weitzer. "Alternatives to Secure Detention and Confinement of Juvenile Offenders." Retrieved July 30, 2010 from U.S. Department of Justice's Office of Juvenile Justice and Delinquency Prevention website: http://www.ncjrs.gov/pdffiles1/ojjdp/208804.pdf.

Bandura, Albert. *Social Learning Theory*. New York, N.Y.: General Learning Press, 1977.

Bentham, Jeremy. *The Panopticon Writings*. Verso Books, 1995.

Brown v. Oneonta (2000).

Bourdieu, Pierre. "The Forms of Capital." J. Richardson [Ed]. *Handbook of Theory and Research for the Sociology of Education*. New York: Greenwood, 1986.

Bourdieu, Pierre. *Masculine Domination*. Stanford, Calif.: Stanford University, 1998.

Bourgois, Philippe. *In Search of Respect: Selling Crack in El Barrio*. New York: Cambridge University Press, 1996.

Buck, Jeff, and Tami Mark. (November 2006). "Youths with Serious Emotional Disturbance: Date from the National Health Interview Survey" *Psychiatric Services*. 57:1573-1582.

Burden, Amanda. "Social Indicators." *City of New York Department of City Planning 2005 Annual Report*.

Bureau of Justice Statistics. "Recidivism in the United States." U.S. Department of Justice, 2009.

Butterfield, Fox. *All God's Children: The Bosket Family and the American Tradition of Violence.* New York: Harper Collins, 1995.

Butterfield, F. (July 12, 1999). "Prisons Brim With Mentally Ill, Study Finds." *NY Times.* P. A2.

Carr, P., Napolitano, L., and Keating, J. (2007). "We Never Call the Cops and Here is Why: A Qualitative Examination of Legal Cynicism in Three Philadelphia Neighborhoods." *Criminology, 45 (2),* pgs. 445- 480.

Clear, Todd R., George F. Cole, and Michael Reisig. *American Corrections* (8th edition). Belmont, Calif.: Thomson Wadsworth, 2009.

Clear, Todd R. "The Problem with 'Addition by Subtraction': The Prison-Crime Relationship in Low-Income Communities." *Invisible Punishment: The Collateral Consequences of Mass Imprisonment.* Edited by Marc Mauer and Meda Chesney-Lind. New York, N.Y.: W.W. Norton & Company, 2002.

Clear, Todd and David R. Karp. *The Community Justice Ideal: Preventing Crime and Achieving Justice.* Boudler, Colo.: Westview Press, 1999.

Coleman, James S. (1988). "Social Capital in the Creation of Human Capital." *The American Journal of Sociology, 94,* pp. S95-S120.

Coleman, Rebecca, Susan Mitchel-Herzfeld, Do Han Kim, and Therese A. Shady. "Long-Term Consequences of Delinquency: Child Maltreatment and Crime in Early Adulthood." *Final Report.* (U.S. Department of Justice: National Institute of Justice, March 31, 2009).

Correctional Association of New York. "Each One Teach One." Retrieved from web site June 2, 2008: www.correctionalassociation.org/JJP/EOTO/EOTO.htm

Correctional Association of New York, The. "Juvenile Detention in New York City: An Annual Report: 2010." Retrieved July 16, 2010, from: http://www.correctionalassociation.org/publications/download/jjp/factsheets/detention_fact_sheet_2010.pdf

Correctional Association of New York. "Rethinking Juvenile Detention in New York City" Produced on March 2002. Retrieved from website on April 21, 2005: http://www.correctionalassociation.org/publications/download/jjp/rethinking_detention.pdf.

Crowley, Keiran. (2008, June 27). "Game Boy Havoc on LI: Teens Busted in 'Grand Theft Auto' Spree." *New York Post.* Retrieved from website: http://www.nypost.com/p/news/regional/item_sZtcRgsjGwMGQ8xNtWJSwI

Daniels, Cora. *Ghetto Nation: A Journey Into the Land of the Bling and the Home of the Shameless.* New York, N.Y.: Random House, Inc., 2007.

Davis, A. (Sept. 1998). "Masked Racism: Reflections on the Prison Industrial Complex." *Color Lines.* p. A1.

Dembart, Lee. (October 6, 1977). "Carter Takes Sobering Trip to South Bronx." *New York Times.* P. A66.

Dewey, John. *Democracy and Education: An Introduction to the Philosophy of Education.* New York, N.Y.: The Macmillan Company, 1916.

DiIulio, John. *Body Count: Moral Poverty and How to Win America's War Against Crime and Drugs.* New York: Simon and Schuster, 1996.

DiIulio, John J. "Reinventing Parole and Probation." *The Brookings Review,* Vol. 15, No. 2 (Spring 1997), pp. 40-42.

Duneier, Mitchell. *Sidewalk.* New York, N.Y.: FSG Books, 1999.

Dworkin, Andrea. *Woman Hating.* New York, N.Y.: E.P. Dutton Books, 1974

Eckholm, Eric. (March 20, 2006). "Plight Deepens for Black Men, Studies Warn." *New York Times.*

Education and Assistance Corporation. Retrieved from website on January 24, 2007: website- http://www.eacinc.org/p-brklnadolfore.htm

Foucault, Michel. *Discipline and Punish: The Birth of the Prison.* New York, N.Y.: Vintage Books, 1977.

Foucault, Michel. "Structuralism and Structures of Knowledge." *Power: Essential Works of Foucault, 1954-1984: Volume 3.* New York: The New Press, 1994/1970.

Frederick, B. (1999). *Factors Contributing to Recidivism Among Youth Placed with New York State Division for Youth* (Research Report, State of New York Criminal Justice Services). Retrieved from Criminal Justice Services website August 3, 2010: http://www.criminaljustice.state.ny.us/crimnet/ojsa/dfy/dfy_research_

Freeman, Joshua B. *Working Class New York.* New York, N.Y.: The Free Press, 2000.

Freire, Paulo. *Pedagogy of the Oppressed* (30th Anniversary Edition). New York, N.Y.: The Continuum International Books, 2000.

Gatto, John Taylor. *The Underground History of American Education.* Oxford, U.K.: Oxford University Press, 2001.

Gelman, A., Fagan, J. and Kiss., A. (2007). "An Analysis of the New York City's Police Department's 'Stop and Frisk' Policy in the Context of Claims of Racial Bias." *Journal of the American Statistical Association,* Vol. 102, No. 479, p. 813-823.

Giordano, Peggy C., Stephen A. Cerkovich, and M.D. Pugh. "Friendships and Delinquency." From *Readings in Juvenile Delinquency and Juvenile Justice.* (Edited by Thomas Calhoun & Constance Chapple). Upper Saddle River, N.J.: Prentice Hall, 2003.

Granack, T.J. "Welcome to the Steel Hotel: Survival Tips for Beginners." From *The Funhouse Mirror,* edited by Robert Gordon Ellis. Pullman, Wash.: Washington State University Press, 2000.

Green, Alan W.C. "'Jim Crow,' 'Zip Coon': The Northern Origins of Negro Minstrelsy." *The Massachusetts Review, Vol. 11, No. 2.* (385-397), 1970.

Hirschi, Travis. "Attachment to Parents." From *Readings in Juvenile Delinquency and Juvenile Justice.* (Edited by Thomas Calhoun & Constance Chapple). Upper Saddle River, N.J.: Prentice Hall, 2003.

hooks, bell. *We Real Cool: Black Men and Masculinity.* New York and London: Routledge, 2004.

Hudson, Edward. (1975, September 17). "Two Policemen Are Slain; East Side Gunman Escapes." *New York Times,* p. A93.

Irwin, John and Donald Cressey. "Thieves, Convicts, and the Inmate Culture." *Social Problems* 10 (1962): 145-157.

Jacobs, Jane. *The Death and Life of Great American Cities.* New York: Random House, 1961.

Jacobson, Michael. *Downsizing Prisons: How to Reduce Crime and End Mass Incarceration.* New York, N.Y.: New York University Press, 2005.

Johnson, Robert. *Hard Time: Understanding and Reforming the Prison.* Belmont, Calif.: Wadsworth, 2002.

Juvenile Justice Center Report. "Adolescence, Brain Development, and Legal Culpability." (January 2004). Retreived from American Bar Association website: http://www.abanet.org/crimjust/juvjus/Adolescence.pdf.

Kaiser, C. (July 20, 1978). "Youth Held in 2 Murders Asked for Placement in Foster Home." *The New York Times,* p. B2.

Kluckholn, Clyde. *Mirror for Man: The Relation of Anthropology to Modern Life.* Phoenix, Ariz.: University of Arizona Press, 1985.

Konty, Mark A., and Charles W. Peek. "Label-Seeking for Status: Peers, Identities, and Domains of Deviance." From *Readings in Juvenile Delinquency and Juvenile Justice.* (Edited by Thomas Calhoun & Constance Chapple). Upper Saddle River, N.J.: Prentice Hall, 2003.

Kozol, Jonathan. *Savage Inequalities: Children in American Schools.* New York: Crown Publishers, 1991.

Kupchik, Aaron. *Judging Juveniles: Prosecuting Adolescents in Juvenile and Adult Courts.* New York: New York University Press, 2006.

Lanier, Mark & Stuart Henry. *Essential Criminology, 2nd Edition.* New York, N.Y.: Westview Press, 2004.

Lasch, Christopher. *The Culture of Narcissism: American Life in an Age of Diminishing Expectations.* New York: W.W. Norton Company, 1979.

Lewis, Oscar. *The Culture of Poverty.* New York, N.Y.: W.H. Freeman, 1966.

Lyon, Larry. *The Community in Urban Society.* Long Grove, Ill.: Waveland Press, 1999.

Majors, Richard and Janet Mancini Billson. *Cool Pose: The Dilemmas of Black Manhood in America.* New York: Lexington Books, 1992.

Martinson, R. (Spring 1974). "What Works?: Questions and Answers About Prison Reform," *The Public Interest,* pp. 22-54.

Matza, David. *Delinquency and Drift.* New Brunswick, N.J.: Transaction Publishers, 1990 (1964).

McNeece, C. Aaron and Sherry Jackson. "Juvenile Justice Policy: Current Trends and 21st Century Issues." *Juvenile Justice Sourcebook: Past, Present and Future.* New York: Oxford University Press, 2004.

Mears, Daniel P., Matthew Ploeger, and Mark Warr. "Explaining the Gender Gap in Delinquency: Peer Influence and Moral Evaluations of Behavior." From *Readings in Juvenile Delinquency and Juvenile Justice.* (Edited by Thomas Calhoun & Constance Chapple). Upper Saddle River, N.J.: Prentice Hall, 2003.

Mennel, Robert. "Origins of the Juvenile Court." Thomas Calhoun and Constance L. Chapple [Eds.] *Readings in Juvenile Delinquency and Juvenile Justice. 3rd Ed.* Upper Saddle River, N.J.: Pearson Education, 2003.

Merton, Robert K. "Opportunity Structure." *On Social Structure and Science.* Chicago, Ill.: University of Chicago Press, 1996.

Merton, Robert K. "Social Structure and Anomie." *On Social Structure and Science.* Chicago, Ill.: University of Chicago Press, 1996.

Moffitt, Terrie E., Avshalom Caspi, Nigel Dickson, Phil Silva, and Warren Stanton (March 8, 1996). "Childhood-onset Versus Adolescent-onset Antisocial Conduct Problems in Males: Natural History from Ages 3 to 18 Years." *Development and Psychopathology,* pp. 399-424.

Neal, Mark Anthony. *New Black Man.* New York, N.Y.: Routledge Press, 2005.

New York City Department of Juvenile Justice. "Building On Success: Next Steps in

New York City Detention Reform." Retrieved on July 21, 2010 from http://www.nyc.gov/html/djj/pdf/detention_reform_action_plan.pdf.

Parascandola, R. and Siemasko, C. (Oct. 8, 2010). "7 From Bronx Gang Latin Kings Goonies nabbed for brutal gay bash attack on man, 2 teens." New York Daily News:http://www.nydailynews.com/news/ny_crime/2010/10/08/2010-1008_7_from_bronx_gang_latin_king_goonies_nabbed_for_brutal_gay_bash_attack_on_man_2_.html

Parenti, Christian. *The Soft Cage: Surveillance in America.* New York, N.Y.: Basic Book, 2003.

Park, Robert. "The City: Suggestions for the Investigation of Human Behavior," *American Journal of Sociology, 20(5),* 1915.

Park, Robert E. and Ernest Burgess. *The City.* Chicago, Ill.: University of Chicago Press, 1925.

Pearl, Arthur. "Cultural and Accumulated Environmental Deficit Models." Richard Valencia [Ed.] *The Evolution of Deficit Thinking: Educational Thought and Practice.* Bristol, Penn.: Falmers Press, 1997.

Petersilia, Joan (1998). "Probation in the United States." *Perspectives, Spring 1998.* Pp. 42-49.

Platt, Anthony. *The Child Savers.* Chicago, Ill.: University of Chicago Press, 1969.

Platt, Anthony. "The Rise of the Child-Saving Movement." *Readings in Juvenile Delinquency and Juvenile Justice. 3rd Ed.(*Upper Saddle River, N.J.: Pearson Education, 2003).

Putnam, Robert. *Bowling Alone: The Collapse and Revival of American Community.* New York: Simon & Schuster Paperbacks, 2000.

Puzzanchere, Charles. "Juvenile Arrests 2008." *Juvenile Justice Bulletin* (U.S. Department of Justice: Office of Juvenile Prevention, Dec. 2009).

Rivera, R., Baker, A., and Roberts, J. (2010, July 11). "A few blocks, 4 years, and 52,000 police stops." *The New York Times, p. A1.*

Roberts, Albert R. *Juvenile Justice Sourcebook: Past, Present and Future.* New York: Oxford University Press, 2004.

Rose, Tricia. *The Hip Hop Wars: What We Talk About When We Talk About Hip Hop—And Why It Matters.* New York, N.Y.: Basic Books, 2008.

Saint-Aubin, Arthur F. "A Grammar of Black Masculinity: A Body of Science." *The Journal of Men's Studies* (March 22, 2002).

Sampson, R., Raudenbush, R., and Earls, F. (1997). "Neighborhoods and Violent Crime: A Multilevel Study of Collective Efficacy." *Science, 277*, pp. 918-924.

Sasha, S.M. (April 2002). "Morbidity in the Ghettos during the Holocaust." *Harefuah—141(4).*

Savolainen, Jukka. "The Impact of Felony ATI Programs on Recidivism." Report by the Criminal Justice Agency: April, 2003.

Scheer, Rebecca. "Keeping Track of New York City's Children: Status Report 2010." New York, N.Y.: Citizens' Committee for Children of New York, Inc., 2010.

Schiebinger, L. *Nature's Body: Gender in the Making of Modern Science.* Boston: Beacon Press, 1993.

Shaw, Clifford R. and Henry D. McKay (May 1932). "Are Broken Homes a Causative Factor in Juvenile Delinquency?" *Social Forces.* Vol. 10, No. 4. Pp. 514-524.

Simons, Ronald, I., Martin G. Miller, and Stephen M. Aigner (1980). "Contemporary

Theories of Deviance and Female Delinquency: An Empirical Test." *Journal of Research in Crime and Delinquency.* 17: 42-57.

Singer, Simon. *Recriminalizing Delinquency: Violent Juvenile Crime & Juvenile Justice Reform.* New York: Cambridge University Press, 1996.

Sloan, Cle (Director). *Bastards of the Party.* HBO Documentary Films, 2006.

Snyder, Howard and Melissa Sickmund. *Juvenile Offenders and Victims: 2006 National Report.* Washington, D.C.: Office of Juvenile Justice and Delinquency Prevention, 2006.

Staples, Robert. *Black Masculinity: The Black Male's Role in American Society.* San Francisco, Calif.: The Black Scholar Press, 1982.

Stowell, Jacob I. and James M. Byrne. "Does What Happens in Prison Stay in Prison? Examining the Reciprocal Relationship between Community and Prison Culture." From *The Culture of Prison Violence.* Boston, Mass.: Pearson Education, 2008.

Sutherland, Edwin and Donald Cressey. *Principles of Criminology.* Lanham, Md.: Alta Mira Press, 1939.

Sutherland, Edwin and Donald R. Cressey. "A Theory of Differential Association." *Criminology,* 8th ed. J.B. Lippincott Company, 1970. Pp. 75-77.

Swidler, Ann (1986). "Culture in Action: Symbols and Strategies." *American Sociological Review* (51), April 273-286.

Tatum, Beverly Daniel. *Why Are All the Black Kids Sitting Together in the Cafeteria?* New York: Basic Books, 1997.

Tilly, Charles. "Contentious Repertoires in Great Britain." [Ed.] Traugott, Mark. *Repertoires & Cycles of Collective Action.* London: Duke University, 1995.

Tonnies, Ferdinand. *Gemeinschaft und Gesellschaft.* [Ed.] Charles P. Loomis. The Michigan State University Press, 1957.

Torbet, Patricia McFall. "Juvenile Probation: The Workhorse of the Juvenile Justice System." Report prepared by the U.S. Department of Justice, Office of Juvenile Justice and Delinquency Prevention, March 1996. Retrieved on October 4, 2010 from OJJDP website: http://www.ncjrs.gov/pdffiles/workhors.pdf.

Travis, Jeremy. *But They All Come Back: Facing the Challenges of Reentry.* Washington, D.C.: The Urban Institute Press, 2005.

United States Department of Justice. "Juvenile Offenders and Victims: 2006 National Report." Retrieved on March 17, 2008 from Office of Justice Programs website: http://www.ojjdp.gov/ojstatbb/nr2006/index.html

United States Federal Bureau of Investigation. *Uniform Crime Report* (2008). Retrieved from FBI website: http://www.fbi.gov/ucr/ucr.htm#cius.

U.S. v. Puerta, 982 F.2d 1297, 1300 (1992).

Vera Institute of Justice, The. "Balancing Punishment and Treatment: Alternatives to Incarceration in New York City." June, 2001. Retrieved March 2, 2005 from Vera Institute website: http://www.vera.org/download?file=75/Balancing%2BATI.pdf.

Wacquant, Loic (2000). "The New Peculiar Institution: On the Prison as Surrogate Ghetto." *Theoretical Criminology.* Vol. 4(3). 377-389.

Wacquant, Loic (1999). "Urban Marginality in the Coming Millenium." *Urban Studies,* Vol. 36 (10), 1639-1647.

Warner, Eric. *The Juvenile Offender Handbook: A Comprehensive Guide to the "J.O. Law" and Related Statutes.* New York: Looseleaf Publications, 2007.

Weaver, Greg S. "Juvenile Delinquency and Drug Use." From *Readings in Juvenile De-*

linquency and Juvenile Justice. (Edited by Thomas Calhoun & Constance Chapple). Upper Saddle River, N.J.: Prentice Hall, 2003.

Weber, Max. "Class, Status, Party." [Ed.] Gerth and Mills: *From Max Weber: Essays in Sociology.* New York: Oxford University Press, 1946.

Wilson, James Q. *Thinking About Crime.* New York: Basic Books, 1983.

Wilson, James and George Kelling. "Broken Windows." *The Atlantic Monthly.* March 1982, pp. 29-38.

Wilson, William Julius. *The Declining Significance of Race: Blacks and Changing American Institutions.* Chicago: University of Chicago Press, 1978.

Wilson, William J. and Loic Wacquant. "The Ghetto Underclass and the Changing Structure of Urban Poverty," from *Quiet Riots: Race and Poverty in the United States.* Westminster, Md.: Random House, 1988.

Wirth, Louis. (1938) "Urbanism as Way of Life." *American Journal of Sociology, 44(1).*

Whren et al v. U.S. (1996).

Index

About the Author

Trevor B. Milton worked with at-risk youth for more than twelve years. Shortly after attaining his bachelor of arts in 1998, he worked with court-involved adolescents in Boston, Massachusetts—and later in New York City—as a case manager, youth counselor, and court advocate. Trevor Milton became interested in research on alternative-to-incarceration programs while he was earning his master of arts in sociology at the New School for Social Research. He earned a Ph.D. in sociology from the New School in 2007. His dissertation was entitled, *The Social Survival Kit: An Exploration of New York City's Community-Based Alternative-to-Incarceration Programs for Juveniles.*

Trevor Milton is currently an assistant professor at the State University of New York—College at Old Westbury. He teaches courses primarily in sociology and criminology. Trevor Milton is also a member of the American Society of Criminology and the American Sociological Association. He continues to be engaged in research on juvenile justice reform, the effects of masculinity on youth crime, and prisoner reentry in New York City.